WOODWORKING PROJECTS *for* WOMEN

By Linda Hendry

An EGW Publishing book—Distributed by Fox Chapel Publishing

Fox
Chapel Publishing

1970 Broad Street • East Petersburg, PA 17520
www.FoxChapelPublishing.com

Woodworking Projects for Women is a compilation of projects originally featured in *Weekend Woodcrafts* magazine. The patterns contained herein are copyrighted by the authors. Artists who purchase this book may make up to three photocopies of each pattern for personal use. The patterns themselves, however, are not to be duplicated for resale or distribution under any circumstances. This is a violation of copyright law.

Publisher	Alan Giagnocavo
Editor	Ayleen Stellhorn
Editorial Assistant	Gretchen Bacon
Cover Design	Jon Deck
Layout	Amy Wiggins, AW Designs

ISBN 1–56523–247–X

Library of Congress Control Number: 2004106145

To order your copy of this book,

please send check or money order

for the cover price plus $3.50 shipping to:

Fox Chapel Publishing

Book Orders

1970 Broad St.

East Petersburg, PA 17520

Or visit us on the Web at **www.FoxChapelPublishing.com**

Printed in China

10 9 8 7 6 5 4 3 2 1

Because working with wood and other materials inherently includes the risk of injury and damage, this book cannot guarantee that creating the projects in this book is safe for everyone. For this reason, this book is sold without warranties or guarantees of any kind, expressed or implied, and the publisher and the authors disclaim any liability for any injuries, losses or damages caused in any way by the content of this book or the reader's use of the tools needed to complete the projects presented here. The publisher and the authors urge all woodworkers to thoroughly review each project and to understand the use of all tools before beginning any project.

Contents

Contents

Introduction

Over the last 40 years, starting when I was a mere child, I was introduced to tools and what they could do. I watched my dad add a couple of rooms onto our house. Wow, some tools and wood and my brothers had more space in their bedroom, plus, we had a huge new family room! I clearly remember watching my grandfather, Papa, laminating Formica to the large eating counter my dad had built. I know he didn't understand why I sat and watched him glue and trim instead of going outside to play. And I'm sure I could not have explained it to him then, but in looking back, I always seemed to need to know how things were done. That hasn't changed. It followed me through Camp Fire Girls and all the crafts my mom taught me. Throughout high school I took mostly art classes and a fun class called Design Workshop where I was taught to use a number of tools and mediums. By my senior year, Dad had built a chess table, and I had decided to make him a walnut and ash chess set using a lathe. Well, I got the walnut side of the set finished in class, then decided to graduate early. But I never forgot the fun I had using that lathe. So, four years later I borrowed a lathe, and for Christmas that year my dad finally got the second half of his chess set!

I was lucky enough to marry a man who was as handy as my dad and my do-it-yourself education has continued for the last 35 years. But watching is just not the same as doing it yourself. When my youngest son was about two, twenty years ago, I started a Christmas boutique with a group of friends and decided to cut my own wood and painting projects. So, I went out and bought myself a band saw. At that time I felt more comfortable using a band saw (it was something like using a sewing machine) and a combination disc and 1" belt sander. For the projects I was making, they were the perfect tools. As with most hobbies though, I ended up having to add to my tools. Soon came the finishing sander, and knowing full well that I would get a lot of use out of it too, I bought my husband a stationary drill press. I was pretty much set. For years I designed and made puzzles and toys for my sons to play with. If they enjoyed the toys, I made more and sold them at the Christmas boutique.

It wasn't until about six years ago that I was fortunate enough to get a job as an associate editor of a woodworking magazine, *Weekend Woodcrafts*. My job includes doing what I love the most: designing, figuring out how a project can work, and using tools to build those designs. When I'm finished with something there is such a feeling of accomplishment. Since starting the job, with the help of my

co-worker, Rob, I have learned how to use, with confidence, more of the tools available out there. Now, among other things, I make grown-up games, shelving, and nursery items for my sons.

In the following pages I will give you a brief explanation of woodworking terms, some differences in woods, tools and their uses, a brief overall of finishing, and above all safety. With each project you accomplish, your confidence will grow and only you can decide how far you'll go in woodworking. The projects in this book are perfect for someone just getting started or for those who want great projects that don't take much time. Read the directions thoroughly beforehand, so you know what tools are involved and the level of difficulty.

I hope this information and the projects in this book start you on your way to a lifetime enjoyment of working in the workshop. Seeing the appreciation on your loved ones' faces when you give them a handcrafted gift is a great reward in and of itself. But making a project that can be handed down through generations gives you a feeling of timelessness. Just be sure to sign and date your project, so your great-grand-daughter knows who made the toy she's playing with.

Happy Woodworking!

Linda Hendry

Wood

Even with all the trees in the world, there are essentially two groups of wood: softwoods and hardwoods.

Softwoods

Softwoods come from conifers, trees that stay green all year and have needles. If you are just starting in woodworking I recommend using softwoods. They are usually easier to find, less expensive, and easier to work with. If you're planning on painting your project, softwoods are the way to go because softwoods are closed grain woods, meaning that they do not have interesting grain patterns that you would want to show off.

The most common softwoods are pine, fir, cedar, and redwood, although this list is likely to vary according to what region you live in. Your local lumber yard or home improvement center should be able to help you find what you want.

Softwoods are cut to standard sizes, but when dried and planed they become smaller. So a 2" x 4" is actually 1½" x 3½". Make sure you take this into account when designing or building a project. It's always a good idea to take a tape measure with you when shopping for wood to be sure of its cut size.

Hardwoods

Hardwoods come from deciduous trees that have leaves and loose them in the fall. Hardwoods are stronger woods, so they are a better choice when building something to last a long time.

Domestic hardwoods, in this case those from America, include oak, maple, cherry, walnut, and poplar. Using one or a combination of these hardwoods will make a great project.

Another category of hardwoods are the imported woods, or exotics, and they are usually much more expensive for that reason. Some of these woods can also be carcinogenic. Find out from your wood source which woods are. To be safe, always wear a dust mask when working with any wood.

Plywoods

Plywood generally comes in 4' x 8' sheets, although you can buy a 4' x 4' sheet in some places. Plywood is made by gluing anywhere from three to nine layers of veneer together. You can purchase plywood with various hardwood faces; oak,

walnut, birch, maple, and many more. This can save you time and money when making larger projects because you won't have to glue-up pieces to get a larger size. For a nice finished look when building with plywood, you will want to cover the edges. This is called face framing. Match the plywood with the same hardwood as the face of the plywood.

Hardboard

Hardboard comes in 4' x 8' sheets. Hardboard is made from pressing together fine wood fibers under heat. There are a few types of hardboard; smooth on one side, smooth on both sides and a tempered hardboard that is harder and darker in color than the others. I like using tempered hardboard for puzzles because it's easy to use and does not splinter. The darker hardboard, also known as masonite, is made with formaldehyde, so make sure you use a dust mask when working with it. The dust can be a problem.

MDF

MDF stands for medium density fiberboard. There are no layers in MDF. It is made from sawdust and resins, which make MDF a very stable product. MDF is heavy, but not very strong. MDF dents and chips easily. Although it paints well, usually MDF is used in a place where it will not be seen. MDF produces a lot of dust when working with it. Wear a mask when working with it.

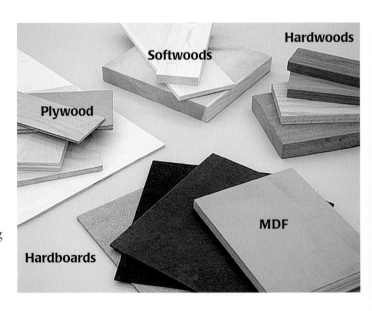

Safety

Being safe in the shop is so important that I can not stress this enough. There are usually several ways to make a cut or round over an edge. Use the tools you have and are comfortable with. Safety is your responsibility. Manufacturers place safety devices on their equipment for your protection. Leave them on. That being said, I want to give you a quick list for safety in your shop.

■ Always have a well stocked first aid kit on hand. Include eyewash and tweezers.

■ Never work alone. Especially when you plan on using power tools. You might need help at some point. If this seems impossible, tell a neighbor, so someone knows and can check on you.

■ Keep your tools and machines in good working condition. Refer to the tools' manuals for maintenance and safety information.

■ Sweep up after yourself. Sawdust is slippery.

■ Put your tools away and keep a neat work space. That way you'll always know where your tools are when you need them.

■ Always wear approved protective eye wear, safety glasses or goggles, when working. A face shield should be worn when turning on a lathe or grinding on a grinder.

■ Wear ear protection. Machines are loud and over time can impair hearing.

■ Never wear loose clothing. It can easily get caught in a tool or machine.

■ Remove your jewelry. As with the clothes, it can get in the way of moving parts.

■ If you have long hair, tie it back. Keep it out of your eyes and away from machinery.

■ Wear closed shoes—no sandals. Protect your feet from falling lumber and tools.

■ Always wear a dust mask when working with wood, or a respirator when sanding or spraying finishes.

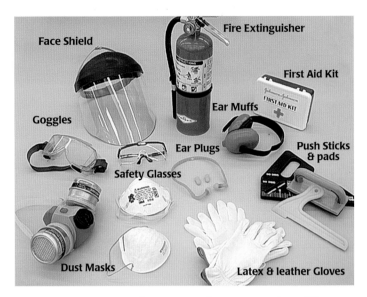

Face Shield · Fire Extinguisher · First Aid Kit · Goggles · Ear Muffs · Ear Plugs · Push Sticks & pads · Safety Glasses · Dust Masks · Latex & leather Gloves

■ Keep an ABC type fire extinguisher in your shop. This kind of fire extinguisher will take care of any kind of fire: (A) wood, trash, and paper, (B) volatile finishing materials, liquid, and grease, (C) electrical equipment.

■ Keep all power cords out from under foot and away from the cutting area. Try not to use extension cords unless absolutely necessary. If you must, make sure they are in good repair, and are of matching amperage (amps).

■ Unplug any machine or tool before changing the blades or bits. You can easily hit the switch and accidently turn it on.

■ Always use push sticks or push blocks. Make sure your hands are safely out of the way.

■ Wear gloves when possible. Leather gloves or a glove with a grip surface are good for moving lumber. Protective latex, tight-fitting gloves are great when staining and painting finished projects.

Before beginning each procedure, think it through: if I push this, where will my hands be? Always remember to wear the proper clothing, to use tools that are in proper working condition, and to read, follow, and understand all the directions that come with your power tools. Above all, pay attention to what you are doing. If your mind is wandering, the shop is not a safe place to be.

Tools

You might already have tools in your garage. If you do you're a lucky one. There are a lot of tools out there and if you are a woodworking novice, it can be a bit overwhelming. I've always been around tools, so I had a passing knowledge of what each tool was used for. If you are unfamiliar with tools and want to learn about them, I suggest buying a book on basic woodworking. Taking classes through your adult-education system or at the local woodworking store is a great way to learn how to properly use a particular tool. And joining a local woodworking club is a great way to meet others as interested in woodworking as you are. Go to woodworking shows when they come to town. There is so much to see and the people to ask questions of are there. Just don't be afraid to ask questions, and ask until you really understand.

Working with wood is a joy, but you have to be comfortable with your tools. One thing I've found in working with tools is that many of the tools are not made for a woman's hand. Our hand span is usually not as wide or long as a mans. So whether you already have tools or you have to buy some, keep this in mind. In choosing your tools, try them "on" for size. We might have to sacrifice power in a battery operated tool to be able to hold it comfortably. Another thing I noticed was that when using a scroll saw on a standard sized stand, my shoulders and neck would get tight and I'd end up sore. I found that at 5'4", I'm not tall enough. So I went back to the shop and made a stool about 6" tall. Now when I work, I stand on the stool and use the whole of my arms, from shoulders to fingertips, when turning work on the scroll saw. There is a lot less strain than before. If you are the only one to use the scroll saw, just make the stand a little shorter to accommodate your height. Another example is the table saw. If you have a portable table saw, then you're probably okay. Portables come with a smaller table surface, so the blade is closer to the front. But a stationary table saw has extended tables, and in that case, you will have to lean over the table a little more. This can get you off balance and that is just not safe. Always use push sticks to keep those hands away from the blade!

I've made up a list of tools from going through the projects in this book. In most cases, there is a portable power tool that can be used in place of a stationary machine. Sometimes the basic hand tool is all you need to use.

This is a list of the tools I think are good to have, stationary or portable, and a brief explanation of what each tool is used for. Tools with a number next to them are what I consider to be basic tools. And although numbers 7 to 10 are not really basic tools, they are great to have. The tools that are not numbered are generally portable tools or hand tools . Once you are familiar with your tools and what they can do, you'll know what will work best for you and your projects.

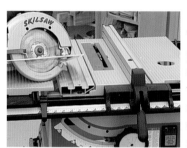

1. Table Saw – (Stationary) The 10" table saw is probably the most common and widely used tool in a wood shop. The table saw is mainly used to make straight cuts with the grain, called ripping. It can also be used in a number of ways to make dadoes, rabbets, grooves, and bevels. Crosscuts can be made with the use of a miter gauge.

Circular Saw – (Portable) A circular saw makes straight cuts with the use of a straight edge and saw horses. Nice to have, but they can be heavy.

2. Drill/Driver – (Portable) A drill/driver is a tool that everyone needs. There are many battery operated models available, along with the corded. These are used to drill holes and to drive screws. Works in the place of the hand-held screwdriver.

Drill Press – (Stationary) The drill press, whether a tall stationary one or the table-top version, is a great tool, although not a necessity. It's easier to drill a straight, more accurate hole when using a drill press. Used for drilling, countersinking, mortising (with an attachment), and sanding, with the addition of a drum sanding bit.

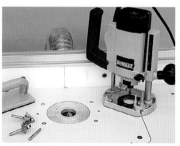

3. Router – (Stationary) The router is a very a useful tool. A router comes separate from the table, but when installed in a router table it is considered a stationary tool.

Routers can put those decorative edges on your piece, round over edges, make rabbets, dadoes, grooves, and chamfers. Now, you can even make biscuit slots with the use of the right bit. If you can get a convertible router, one that can go from a standard router to a plunge router, you'll be able to do almost anything.

Plunge Router – (Portable) We show using a portable plunge router for making hanging slots. This can be done with a router table; just plan ahead and make the slot before any curves are cut on the piece. It's much easier to have a straight edge to hold against the fence.

4. Band Saw – (Stationary) The band saw is used mainly to cut curves. The smaller the width of the blade, the tighter the curve. Band saws can cut thicker wood than a scroll saw or a jigsaw. And with a wide blade installed you can use a band saw to re-saw thicker lumber to get thinner pieces, saving on the cost of lumber.

5. Scroll Saw – (Stationary) A scroll saw is good for making inside cuts in projects (the band saw cannot do this). It works well on smaller pieces, but is limiting in the thickness of wood used, usually nothing over 1" thick.

Saber Saw – (Portable) The saber saw, also known as a jig saw, is an alternative to use when cutting curves, if the curves are not too small. It's good to use a saber saw on larger projects where using a stationary tool would not be safe.

6. Finishing Sander – (Portable) Although called a finishing sander, this type of sander can take you through all grits of sandpaper. My favorite is an orbital sander. It fits the hand well, and there's more control.

7. Biscuit Joiner – (Portable) The biscuit joiner is a great tool for joining wood together. The biscuit joiner cuts a slot. With the addition of a store-bought biscuit and glue, you have a good strong joint along the butted edges of two pieces.

8. Brad Nailer – (Portable) A brad nailer is fun and fast. Brad nailers come in various sizes, and are either electric or pneumatic (used with an air compressor). Size will depend on your type of projects. But one that can accommodate several sizes of brads is best.

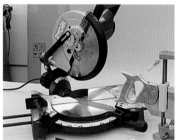

9. Miter Saw – (Portable) A miter saw is used mainly for cutting angles. They are also used to cut across the grain for wood length. There are several types: a basic miter saw that makes straight cuts and angles, or a compound miter saw where the blade not only pivots, but also tilts.

Miter Box with Saw – (Hand Tool) A miter box is a small table-top tool used with a hand saw that usually comes as a set. It can be as simple as a wooden box with angles cut in it, or a larger one made of metal. A miter box and saw can cut angles, just not as accurately or as fast as a larger miter saw.

10. Planer – (Stationary) A planer is used to shave down the thickness of the wood. For example, a ¾" stock can be planed to achieve a ½"- ¼" thickness, which gives you much more flexibility when building projects. Re-sawing on a band saw and sanding smooth is an option in some cases.

I suggest buying the best tool you can afford at the time. Take into consideration how much work you expect to do with it. There are essentially two lines of power tools. One is for the home do-it-yourselfer, and one is for the professional. As you gain experience you'll know what to look for in the tools you need.

Supplies

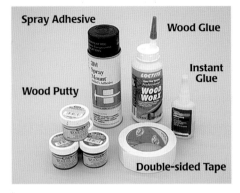

Spray Adhesive
Wood Glue
Instant Glue
Wood Putty
Double-sided Tape

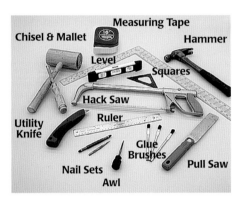

Measuring Tape
Chisel & Mallet
Hammer
Level
Squares
Hack Saw
Utility Knife
Ruler
Glue Brushes
Pull Saw
Nail Sets
Awl

Pipe Clamp
Web Clamp
Bar Clamps
Spring Clamp
Wooden Handscrew Clamp

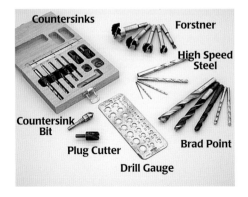

Countersinks
Forstner
High Speed Steel
Countersink Bit
Plug Cutter
Brad Point
Drill Gauge

While the power tools are necessary, there are other tools and supplies that are frequently used on all projects. It's a good idea to keep these on hand too:

1. **First-aid kit** – basics, along with eye wash and tweezers.

2. **Fire Extinguisher** – for type ABC fires. (A) wood, trash, and paper, (B) volatile finishing materials, liquid, and grease, (C) electrical equipment

3. **Double-sided Tape** – to adhere patterns or gang wood together before cutting or drilling.

4. **Wood Glue** – sets up faster than white glue. Comes in dark color for darker woods.

5. **Instant Glue** – for wood-on-wood or wood-on-metal adhesion.

6. **Spray Adhesive** – keeps patterns on wood when scroll sawing.

7. **Wood Putty** – fills nail holes before finishing.

8. **Awl** – great for marking hole locations. The mark left from the awl will keep the drill from wandering.

9. **Steel Ruler** – a reliable ruler is a must.

10. **Nail Set** – a tool used to set the nail under the surface of the wood.

11. **Hammer** – a must in any shop.

12. **Chisel and Mallet** – to square or clean up corners after routing.

13. **Square** – keeping things square is important.

14. **Measuring Tape** – easy to keep handy for those longer pieces.

15. **Hack Saw** – needed to cut metal rods.

16. **Glue Brushes** – to spread glue on larger surfaces.

17. **Utility Knife** – good all purpose tool.

18. **Pull saw** – to trim dowels flush.

19. **Clamps** – you can never have enough clamps. Get a variety of sizes and styles (bar, pipe, spring, web).

20. **Wooden Handscrew Clamp** – great for holding small pieces when drilling without marring the wood.

21. **Drill Bit Set** – a good set of drill bits in a variety of sizes. Brad point and forstners are good. A drill gauge helps determine diameters.

22. **Countersink Bit** – used to countersink a hole so the screw head will set under the surface of the wood. A plug cutter to cut plugs for the countersunk holes.

23. **Scissors** – for cutting patterns, tape, etc.

24. **Sandpaper** – 80, 100, 150, 220 grits for a good variety.

Joints

Preparing the Surface

Butt Joint – Butt joints are the simplest way to attach two pieces of wood together. There are three types of butt joints: the face-to-face, end-to-edge, and the end-to-face.

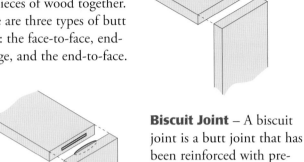

Biscuit Joint – A biscuit joint is a butt joint that has been reinforced with pre-made wooden biscuits that are glued into slots milled into each piece of wood.

Dowel Joint – A dowel joint is a butt joint that has been reinforced with small round wooden pegs or dowels that are glued into holes drilled into each pice of wood.

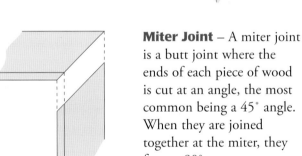

Miter Joint – A miter joint is a butt joint where the ends of each piece of wood is cut at an angle, the most common being a 45° angle. When they are joined together at the miter, they form a 90° corner.

Lap Joint – A lap joint is achieved by cutting away half of the thickness or width of two boards so that when they are put together the surfaces are flush.

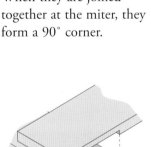

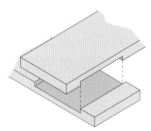

In working with wood you will probably find that there is one favorite aspect of the process that you will love—the creating, seeing all the pieces come together and the project take shape. Then there will be the least favorite part of the process. I think for most people that would be sanding. It can be dusty, dirty and boring. But without a well prepared surface all your other hard work will have been a waste of time.

Whenever possible sand pieces before assembly. This way you'll be able to get to the edges that will become hard to reach spots when assembled.

Filling – If you have used any brads or finishing nails, use a nail set to set the nails below the surface of the wood. Sometimes there will be places where the pieces just don't line up perfectly. If you are going to paint the project, wood putty can be used to fill very small areas. If you were planning on staining or oiling, the filler will have to match. Putty does come in different colors. A tip I learned from my dad was to use the sawdust from the project. Clean out the sander's collection bag before sanding the project, that way you will have matching sawdust. Then mix a little white glue with the sawdust to make a paste and fill holes using this mixture. The white glue will dry clear, so all you'll see is the same color as the project wood. Now remember, this will only work if the space is very small. When the putty or paste is dry you are ready to sand.

Sanding – A good finishing sander, my favorite is an orbital, can sand most projects, although, a little hand-sanding is usually always needed.

Always wear a dust mask when sanding. If possible, hook your sander up to a portable Shop Vac or vacuuming system. This will save a lot of clean up and protect your lungs. Always sand through a sequence of grits. If your wood is rough, start sanding with an 80-grit (coarse) sandpaper. On smoother surfaces, you can start with a 120-grit (medium) or a 150-grit (fine), then move onto a 220-grit (very fine) for the final sanding.

Always sand with the wood grain to prevent scratches.

Use a tack rag to remove any dust before painting. Vacuum the dust off a project if you are going stain or oil, as the tack rag may leave a slight residue that would prevent even penetration of stain or oil.

Finishes

There are so many finishes available on the market. The type of finish you choose will usually depend on the look you're going after. In most instances when something is made of a softwood, such as pine, I will paint it. Hardwoods are so beautiful that you really don't want to hide the great wood grains, so I like to either oil or stain and seal a hardwood project.

Staining and Oiling – There are both exterior and interior varnishes depending on where your project will be used. Think about what your project is going to be used for. If it's a child's toy and you want a natural finish, then a child-safe finish like mineral oil is required. Do not use vegetable oil, it will go rancid. I generally use a spray water-based polyurethane on toys. And although a finish is usually considered toxic only in its liquid form and fine when dry, it's always better to be safe than sorry. Think ahead and you shouldn't have any problems.

Apply a wood conditioner before staining. End grains and softwoods absorb stain differently so using a wood conditioner will give you a more uniform finish.

Finishes such as varnish, polyurethane, and laquer will build up a protective shield on the surface of the wood and are considered surface finishes. For resisting stains and scratches, a surface finish is better than a penetrating finish. Surface finishes come with either a solvent-base or water-base. Water-base finishes are non-toxic and non-flammable. Draw-backs to the water-based finishes are that they will tend to raise the grain of the wood and may not be compatible with oil-based stains and fillers.

A penetrating finish like oil will be absorbed into the wood, and harden within the wood's fibers. A penetrating finish gives a soft sheen that emphasizes the grain on a project. Oils come in different colors.

My best tip for finishing would be to read all manufacturer labels thoroughly and always follow the manufacturer's instructions. And take note of air temperature, as it will make a big difference in how a finish cures.

Gel Stain · Spray Polyurethane · Danish Oil · Wood Conditioner · Mineral Oil · Enamel Paints · Penetrating Stain · Acrylic Paints · Child Safe Finish

Painting – Painting a project is a great way to personalize it, especially children's projects. Take into consideration how heavily used the object will be. There are different types of paints, among them acrylics, latex enamels, and oil enamels. I try to stay away from the oils. The latex paints have come such a long way in recent years that there is really no reason to put up with the smell and longer drying time associated with oil based paints.

On smaller items I like to use acrylic paints from the hobby store. They don't cost much, and come in a wide variety of colors. For the larger projects, like the seaside bench in this book where I wanted a specific look, I will go to the hardware store and look for a kit or system designed to give me that look. Just remember to seal all your painting. The sealer is what will make your project last. Remember to read and follow all the manufacturer's instructions.

Ladies' Tool Rack

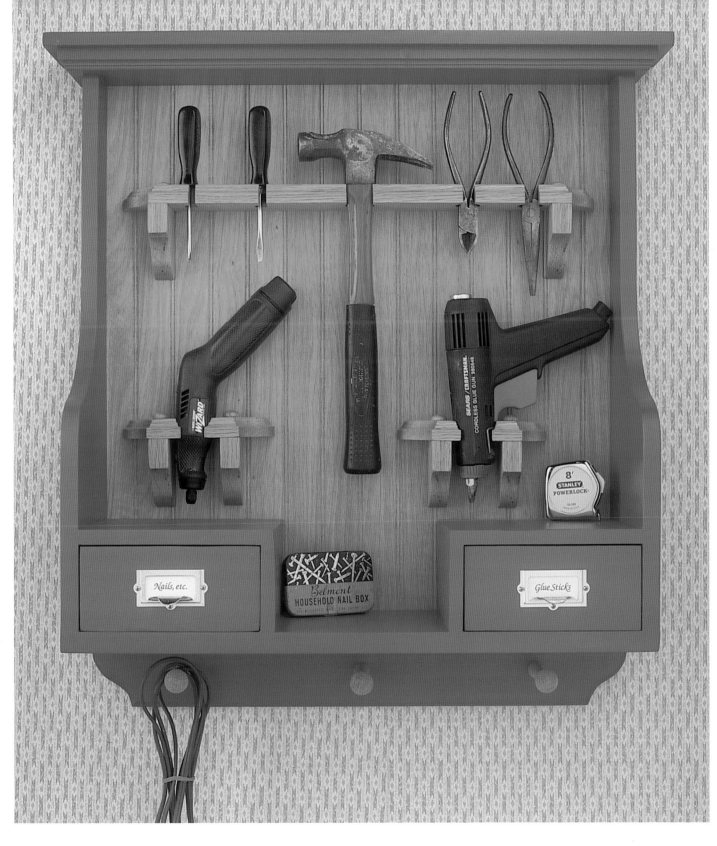

Material List

		T x W x L
A	back (1) (oak beaded board paneling)	¼" x 21" x 21"
B	side (2) (pine)*	¾" x 6" x 21"
C	bottom (1) (pine)	¾" x 6" x 21½"
D	top (#1) (1) (pine)	¾" x 3" x 23"
E	top (#2) (1) (pine)	½" x 3½" x 24"
F	bottom face (for pegs) (1) (pine)	¾" x 3" x 21½"
G	drawer side casing (2) (pine)	¾" x 5⅝" x 3"
H	drawer top casing (2) (pine)	½" x 5⅝" x 7"
I	drawer front (2) (pine)	½" x 2⅞" x 6⅜"
J	drawer sides (4) (pine)	½" x 2⅞" x 4½"
K	drawer back (2) (pine)	½" x 2⅞" x 6⅜"
L	drawer bottom (2) (plywood)	¼" x 5¾" x 5"
M	upper rack (1) (oak)*	¾" x 2" x 19"
N	lower racks (2) (oak)*	¾" x 2" x 6"
O	brackets (6) (oak)*	¾" x 2" x 2⅝"

Supply List

P	Forstner bits (5)	½", 1", 1⅛", 1⅝", 1¾"
Q	cove and bead router bit	1¼"
R	wood screws	#6 x 1¼", #6 x 1⅝"
S	brad nailer	1"
T	pegs (3) (oak)	3" x ½" diam.
U	drawer pulls (2)	1¼" x 2½"
V	oak buttons (6)	½" diam.

*See Pattern Packet.

Rabbet

Step 1 - Cut the side blanks (B) to the dimensions given in the material list. Using a ⅜" rabbeting bit, rout a ¼"-deep rabbet along the back inside edge of the side blanks by standing the blank on its edge as shown.

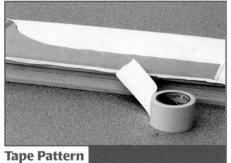

Tape Pattern

Step 2 - Tape the two side blanks together using double-sided tape and affix the pattern (B) to the ganged blanks. Make sure the rabbeted edge is flush with the back edge of the pattern.

Cut Profiles

Step 3 - Using a bandsaw or scroll saw, cut the side profiles.

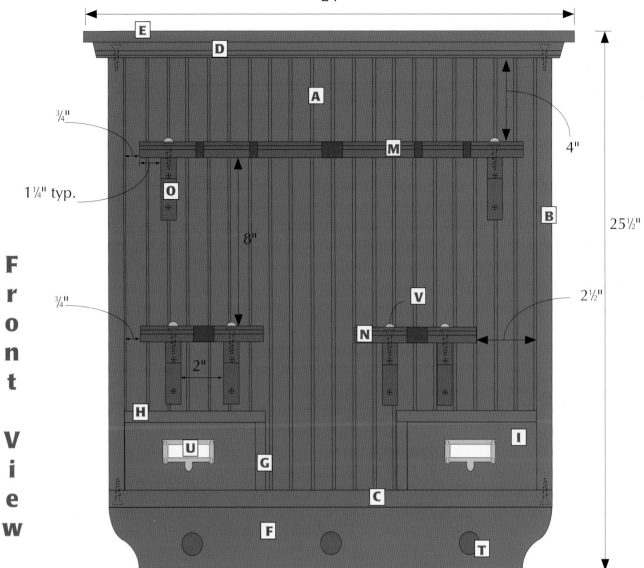

24"

E
D
A
M
O
B
H
V
N
U
G
I
C
F
T

3/4"

1¼" typ.

3/4"

8"

2"

4"

25½"

2½"

Front View

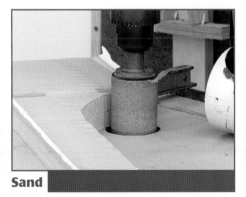

Sand

Step 4 - While the sides are still taped togeth-er, use a drum sander to sand the edges smooth as shown. Separate the two sides and set aside.

Chisel

Step 5- Cut the back (A), the two tops (D, E) and the bottom (C) to the dimensions given in the material list.

Measure in 1" from each end on both the top (D) and bottom (C) blanks. This will give you a starting and stopping point for routing. Using the ⅜" rabbeting bit, rout a ¼" rabbet along one edge of the blanks. Do not turn these pieces on their edge.

Use a chisel and mallet to clean up the ends of the rabbets as shown.

Rout

Step 6 - Rout the front and side edges of the top (D), using the 1¼" cove and bead router bit (Q) as shown.

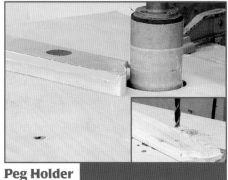

Peg Holder

Step 7 - Cut the bottom face blank (F) to the dimensions given in the material list. Using double-sided tape, affix the pattern. Use a bandsaw to cut the profile and sand using the drum sander as shown. Transfer the hole markings to the wood with a center punch. Rout the bottom and side edges with the cove and bead bit (Q). With a ½" drill bit in the drill press, drill holes on marks as shown. Sand all pieces through 220-grit sandpaper.

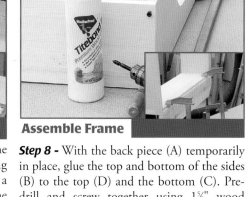

Assemble Frame

Step 8 - With the back piece (A) temporarily in place, glue the top and bottom of the sides (B) to the top (D) and the bottom (C). Pre-drill and screw together using 1⅝" wood screws (R). Clamp.

Attach the peg holder (F) with glue and use a 1" brad nailer to nail through the bottom (C) into the peg holder. Center the top (E) to top (D). Glue and nail together.

Drawer Casings

Step 9 - Cut the side drawer casings (G) and the top drawer casings (H) to the dimensions given in the material list. Glue and nail at a 90-degree angle the top casing onto the side casing. Using a block the same height as the side piece for a spacer, glue and nail in place as shown. Clamp.

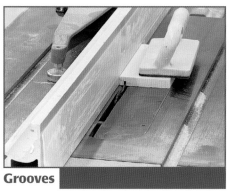

Grooves

Step 10 - Cut the drawer blanks (I, J, K, L) to the dimensions given in the material list. With a ¼" dado blade set to a height of ¼" in the table saw, cut a groove ½" in from the bottom edge on the blanks (I, J, K), as shown.

Assemble Drawer

Step 11 - To assemble the drawers, glue the front (I) to the sides (J). Slide the drawer bottom (L) in place and glue the back (K) to the sides. Nail in place from the front and back into the sides. Fill nail holes with wood filler. Sand when dry.

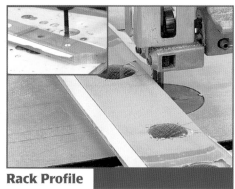

Rack Profile

Step 12 - For the upper and lower racks (M, N), repeat the directions given in Steps 2 and 3, using the patterns for the racks (M, N). Drill, using the Forstner bits (P), following the sizes indicated on the patterns. Using the bandsaw, follow the cutting lines on the pattern and cut the access for the tools. Check the tools you will be hanging for any placement adjustments needed.

Brackets

Step 13 - Cut the brackets (O) to the dimensions given in the material list. Gang tape two bracket blanks together as shown. Tape the bracket pattern to the blanks. Gang cut the bracket profiles using the bandsaw. Sand. Finish the oak pieces with several coats of Watco Oil. The pine is painted with Colonial Red acrylic latex paint. Let dry.

Attach Racks

Step 14 - Assemble by nailing the back (A) onto the frame using the 1" brad nailer.

To assemble the racks, line up the brackets with the front corners on the racks as shown in the inset photo. Countersink for the oak buttons (V) and pre-drill to attach the brackets to the racks using wood screws #6 x 1¼" (R).

Screw the racks through the back as shown. Refer to the drawing for placement. Place the oak buttons over the screw heads.

Finishing

Step 15 - Center and screw the drawer pulls (U) to the front of the drawers. Attach pegs (T) to the bottom face (F). Using a hanging slot bit in the router, rout two slots on both back side edges of the cabinet.

Scrapbook

Laminate

Step 1 - Laminate enough hardwood layers to achieve a 1½" thickness for the cover strip (C). Clamp and let dry.

Cut Strip

Step 2 - Using a table saw, cut a strip ⅜" wide. Cut the cover strip to the length given in the material list.

Mark Holes

Step 3 - Mark holes for the Chicago bolts (D) on the cover strip. Measure 5¹⁵⁄₁₆" down from the top for the center hole, ⅜" in from the inside edge of the strip. Measure up 1¹¹⁄₁₆" from each end for the two other holes, again ⅜" in from the inside edge.

Cut Widths

Step 4 - Plane enough wood for the front cover (A) and the back cover (B). Using a table saw, cut the covers to the width given in the material list.

Material List	T x W x L
A front cover (1) (walnut)	⅜" x 9" x 11⅞"
B back cover (1) (walnut)	⅜" x 10½" x 11⅞"
C cover strip (1) (laminated hardwoods)	⅜" x 1½" x 11⅞"
Supply List	
D Chicago bolts (3) #00K40.05*	30-36mm
E decorative hinges (3) (brass)	1⁵⁄₁₆" x 2¼"
F drill bits	¼", ⁷⁄₆₄"
G hack saw	
H Watco Danish Oil	
I cover plate (self-sticking gold tone)	2½" x 3"

*This item is available from Lee Valley & Veritas hardware catalog.
For more information, call (800) 871-8158 or e-mail **www.leevalley.com.**

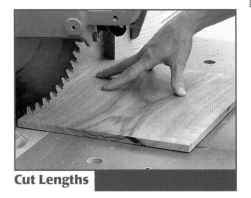

Cut Lengths

Step 5 - Cut both covers to the length given in the material list using a radial arm saw.

decorative hinge

1½"

⅜"

Side View

10½"

Gang Strip and Back

Step 6 - Lining up the outside edges, gang together the back cover and the cover strip using double-sided tape.

Drill Holes

Step 7 - With a ¼" drill bit (F) in the drill press, drill through the ganged pieces where previously marked on the strip.

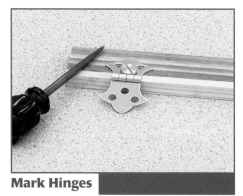

Mark Hinges

Step 8 - Place the screw portion of the Chicago bolts (D) through the center hole of the hinges and mark with an awl the remaining holes for the hinge screws.

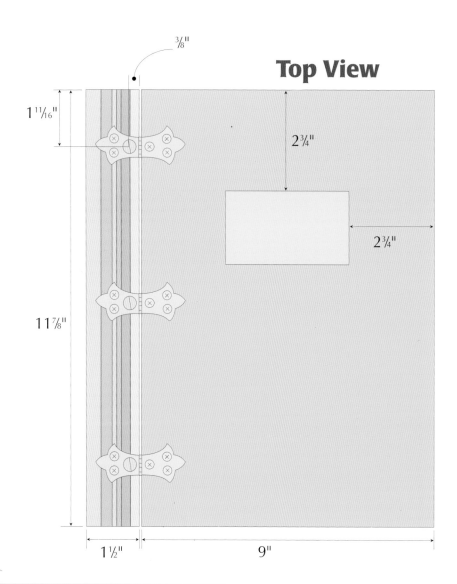

Top View

3/8"

1¹¹⁄₁₆"

2¾"

2¾"

11⅞"

1½"

9"

Attach Hinges

Step 9 - Using the ⁷⁄₆₄" drill bit (F), pre-drill the holes for the hinge screws.

Remove the Chicago bolts and sand through 220-grit sandpaper.

Finish with several coats of Watco Danish Oil (H). Let dry.

Pre-drill and attach the hinges (E) to the front cover with the screws. (You will probably have to cut down the screws to ¼". Use a hack saw (G) and a vise to hold the screws while cutting.)

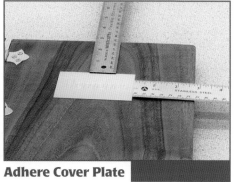

Adhere Cover Plate

Step 10 - Thread the Chicago bolt post through the back cover and add scrapbook pages. Set the front cover on top and screw the Chicago bolt screws into the posts.

If you are using a cover plate (I), refer to the drawing above for placement.

Hanging Night Stand

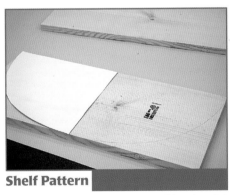

Shelf Pattern

Step 1 - Cut the shelf (A), shelf bracket (B) and shelf backing (C) to the dimensions given in the material list.

Locate the shelf pattern. Trace the pattern onto one side of the shelf; then flip the pattern over and trace the remaining half profile. Repeat steps for second shelf.

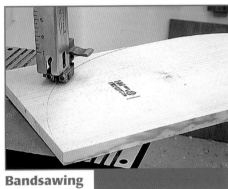

Bandsawing

Step 2 - Use the bandsaw to cut the shelf profile out. Use the drum sander to smooth the cuts.

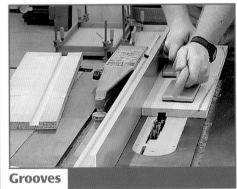

Grooves

Step 3 - Use the table saw to make a ¾"-wide by ⅜"-deep through groove in both the shelf backing blanks. Start the grooves 1½" down from the top edge.

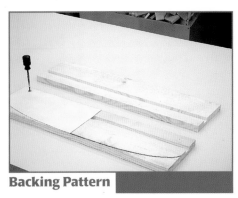

Backing Pattern

Step 4 - Locate the shelf backing pattern and trace onto each piece. Trace the pattern on one side; then flip pattern to trace opposite side. Use an awl to mark the two screw hole locations.

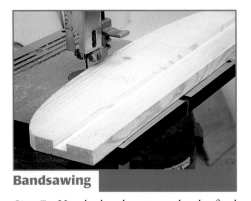

Bandsawing

Step 5 - Use the bandsaw to make the final profile of the shelf backing. Use the drum sander to smooth the cuts.

Material List	T x W x L
A shelf (2) (pine)*	¾" x 11¼" x 24"
B shelf bracket (2) (pine)*	1½" x 8" x 9"
C shelf backing (2) (pine)*	¾" x 6" x 24"
D wood plugs (2)	⅜" diam. x ⅜"
Supply List	
E buttons (4)	½"
F wood screws with plastic mollies	#6 x 2"
G wood screws (14)	#6 x 2"
H double-sided tape	
I J.W. Etc., White Lightning stain and sealer	

*See Pattern Packet.

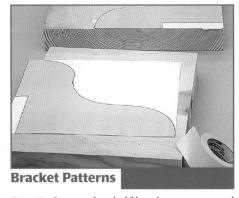

Bracket Patterns

Step 6 - Locate the shelf bracket pattern and make two copies. Adhere a copy to each blank with double-sided tape (H).

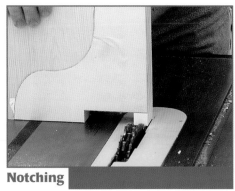

Notching

Step 7 - Use the table saw with the ¾" dado blade raised to a height of ¾" to remove the material that is located on the pattern.

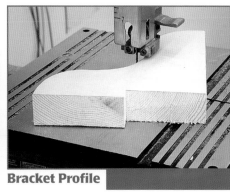

Bracket Profile

Step 8 - Use the bandsaw to cut the shelf brackets out. Use the drum sander to smooth the cuts.

Countersinking

Step 9 - The shelf is held to the backing with five evenly spaced 2" wood screws (G). Space the screw locations on the back side of the backing and down the center of the groove. Use a #8 countersink bit to pre-drill each location. Only countersink enough to flush the screw heads.

Shelf Countersink

Step 10 - The shelf is attached to the shelf bracket with one 2" wood screw (G). Locate the center of the shelf and measure up 5¼". Use the #8 countersink bit to pre-drill and countersink enough to use a wood plug (D) to cover screw head.

Button Locations

Step 11 - Use the drill press with the #10 countersink bit to make a ½"-wide hole at each corner of the shelf backing. Drill to a depth deep enough for the buttons to sit flush. The location of each hole is located on the pattern.

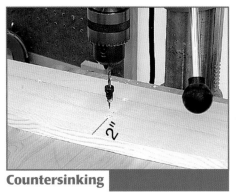

Countersinking

Step 12 - The shelf bracket is attached to the shelf backing with a 2" wood screw (G). Locate the center of the shelf backing and measure up 2" on the back side from the bottom edge. Use the #8 countersink bit to pre-drill into the shelf backing.

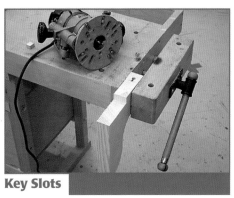

Key Slots

Step 13 - A keyhole slot is milled into each of the shelf brackets. On the short section of the bracket, the part that comes in contact with the wall gets the keyhole slot. Start the key slot 1" up from the bottom edge. Make the slot ½" long. Use the plunge router and the work bench vise to make the slot.

Ogee Bit

Step 14 - Sand the entire project through 220-grit sandpaper.

Use a decorative ogee bit and rout the shelf's top edge, stopping and starting ⅜" from both ends.

Exploded View

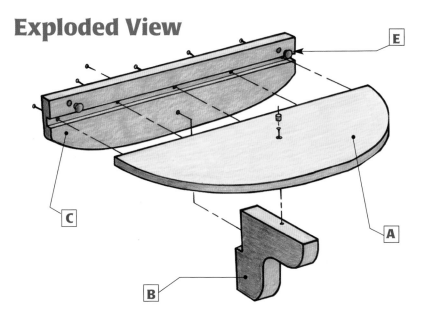

Side View

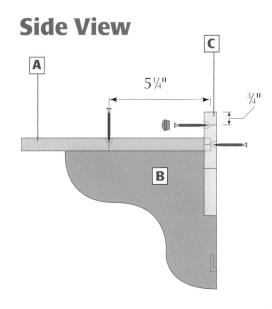

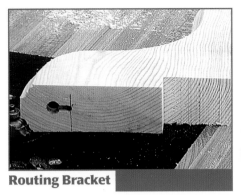

Routing Bracket

Step 15 - Use the same ogee bit to rout the edges of the shelf brackets.

Shelf Assembly

Step 16 - Use the 2" wood screws (G) to fasten the shelf to the shelf backing. Pre-drill all screw locations.

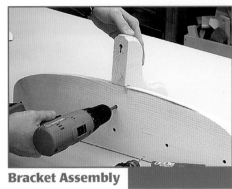

Bracket Assembly

Step 17 - Use the 2" wood screws (G) to attach the shelf brackets to the shelf backing and shelf.

Plug Cutting

Step 18 - Use the drill press and a ⅜" plug cutting bit to make the two wooden plugs for the shelves.

Plug Assembly

Step 19 - Glue the wooden plugs into the shelves. Use a wooden mallet to secure each plug. Cut the plugs flush and sand.

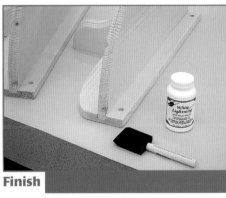

Finish

Step 20 - The finish on this project is a white-wash. J.W. Etc. supplied the wash that comes as a sealer too. When hanging the shelves, if studs in the wall are not usable, be sure to use the plastic mollies and screws (F) in securing the project to the wall.

Top View

Front View

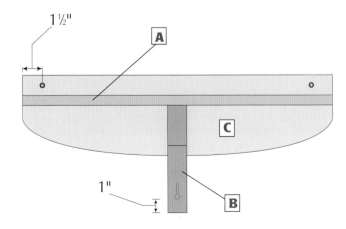

1 ½"

1"

Book Lamp

Routing the Edges

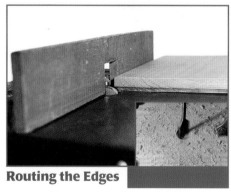

Step 1 - Cut the base (A) to the dimensions in the material list. Rout the edges with a ½" cove bit. Find the center of the base. Drill a hole on the underside of the base at this center point for the lamp assembly. First, drill a counterbored hole ½" deep with a 1⅛" spade bit. Then, drill through the bottom with a ¹³⁄₃₂" bit. Sand base smooth through 220-grit sandpaper.

Adding the Feet

Step 2 - On the underside of the base, measure in ⅞" from both sides of each corner and mark. Drill a ¼" hole, ½" deep, to attach the drawer pull feet. Enlarge the hole in the drawer pulls (H) with a ¼" drill bit, drilling the hole ½" deep. Attach the drawer pull feet to the base with glue and dowels (G). Clamp together and set aside to dry.

Cutting the Binding

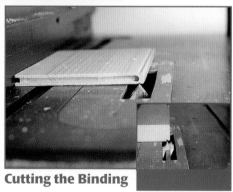

Step 3 - Cut all the books (B, C, D, E and F) to the dimensions. The binding grooves are made with moulding cutters. The thicker books are edged with a ¼" bead cutter. Adjust the saw fence so that only the edge of the cutter is used to give a single bead, approximately ¼". To give the books an aged look, move the cutter in another ¼" and round over the excess wood by hand. The thin ½" book (D) is cut with a 90-degree flute cutter. Set the depth of both cutters to approximately ⅛".

Material List	T x W x L
A base (1) (oak)	¾" x 8½" x 11"
B book (1) (pine)	1½" x 7" x 9"
C book (1) (pine)	¾" x 6" x 8½"
D book (1) (pine)	½" x 5½" x 8"
E book (1) (pine)	1½" x 4¼" x 7½"
F book (1) (pine)	¾" x 3½" x 7"

Supply List	
G ¼" dowel (4) (oak)	1"
H wooden drawer pulls (4) (oak)	1" x 1½" x 1½"
I socket (1) (brass finish)	
J cord set (1) (brown)	8'
K threaded pipe (1)	¾" x 36"
L brass tubing (1)	⅜" x 36"
M large brass neck (1)	¹⁵/₁₆" x 1¹⁵/₁₆"
N small brass neck (1)	¹¹/₁₆" x ⁷/₁₆"
O knurled nut (1) (brass)	¾"

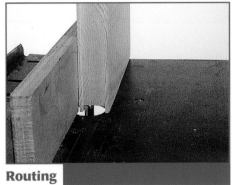

Routing

Step 4 - The other three edges of the books need to be recessed to give the cover an ⅛" overhang over the pages. A ½" straight cutting router bit is used to cut the thicker books (B, C, E, F). A ¼" bit is used to make the recess in the thin ½" book (D). The recesses are cut ¼" deep. To cut the recesses, position the router fence so the cover thickness is ⅛". The cuts on the vertical edge can be made straight through, but a stop block will be needed on the horizontal edges. Be careful not to remove too much material near the binding. Clean up and round the ends near the binding with a sharp utility knife.

Drilling Holes

Step 5 - Find the center of each book by drawing diagonal lines from opposite corners. Drill a ¹³/₃₂" through the center of each book. Sand all books smooth through 220-grit sandpaper.

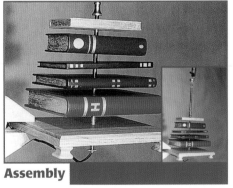

Assembly

Step 6 - Paint the books with acrylic paints. The page edges were painted with DecoArt textured metallic gold paint. When paint is dry, seal books with matte spray sealer. Then wax books with J.W. Etc.'s Finishing Wax.

Connecting the Lamp

Step 7 - To assemble, stack books as desired on top of base and insert threaded pipe (K) through holes. Thread knurled nut (O) onto bottom of threaded pipe. Pull cord set (J) through the threaded pipe so that the wire ends extend out the top of the pipe. Place the large brass neck (M), the brass tubing (L) and the small brass neck (N) over the threaded tube. Insert the wires through the bottom of the brass socket (I). Tie the wire ends in an underwriter's knot to provide strain relief. Connect the smooth wire to the gold screw on the socket. Connect the ribbed wire to the silver screw on the socket. Push the socket back together, tucking the wires inside. Pull the lamp together, and tighten the knurled nut snug. Attach a bulb and a matching lamp shade and plug in your masterpiece.

Underwriter's Knot

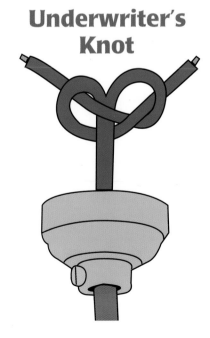

Victorian Shelf

Laminate for Thickness

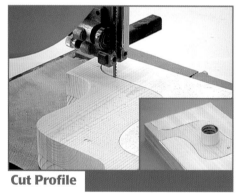

Cut Profile

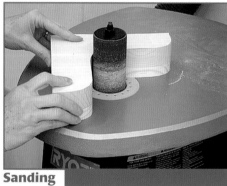

Sanding

Step 1 - Laminate, if necessary, to achieve the 2" thickness required for the shelf brackets (A). We laminated ¾"- and 1½"- thick boards together. Plane to achieve the 2" thickness given in the material list.

Step 2 - Locate the bracket pattern. Make a copy since you will need two patterns. Adhere the patterns to the bracket blank using double-sided tape (D) as shown in the inset.

Using a bandsaw, cut around each bracket along the pattern lines.

Step 3 - Using a drum sander, sand the curved edges of the brackets to remove any kerf marks.

Rout Brackets

Step 4 - With a cove router bit (E) in the router table set to a depth of ³⁄₁₆," rout the two outside edges of the brackets.

Rout Shelf

Step 5 - Cut the shelf (B) to the dimensions given in the material list. Place a decorative router bit (F) in the router table, and rout only the two top ends and the top front edge of the shelf.

Material List	T x W x L
A shelf brackets (2) (pine)*	2" x 8" x 8½"
B shelf (pine)	¾" x 10" x 36"
Supply List	
C finials (2)	1⅞" x 4½"
D double-sided tape	
E cove router bit	³⁄₁₆"
F decorative router bit (your choice)	
G biscuits (4)	#10
H hanging slot router bit	
I dowel screws (2)	¼" x 2"
J wood glue	
K drill bit	¹⁵⁄₆₄"
L McCloskey Special Effects paint	
M vise grips	

*See Pattern Packet.

Center Marks on Shelf

Step 6 - To mark the bracket placement, turn the shelf upside down, and measure in 2" from each end. Mark as shown in the inset. Draw the line the length of the bracket.

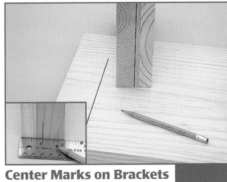

Center Marks on Brackets

Step 7 - Make a center line mark on the back of the shelf brackets as shown in the inset. Continue the line along the top edge of the bracket.

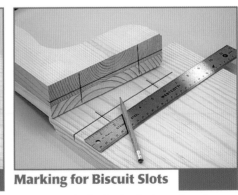

Marking for Biscuit Slots

Step 8 - With the backs flush, make a line on both the bracket and shelf at 2" and 6" in from the back edge.

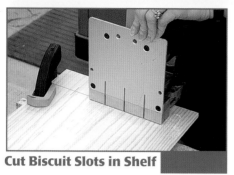

Cut Biscuit Slots in Shelf

Step 9 - Clamp the shelf and, using a biscuit joiner set for a #10 biscuit, cut the biscuit slots where marked.

Side View

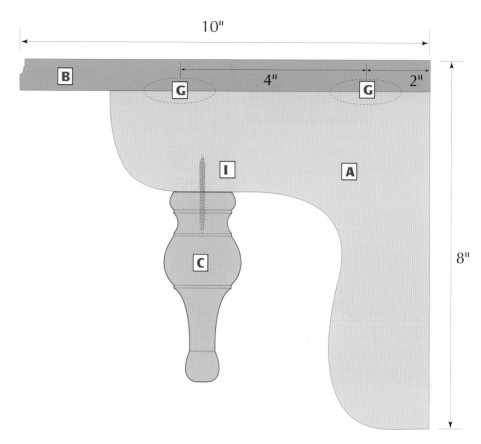

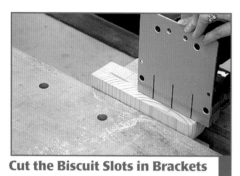

Cut the Biscuit Slots in Brackets

Step 10 - With the shelf bracket firmly clamped, cut the biscuit slots in the brackets where previously marked.

Mark for Hanging Slots

Step 11 - To mark for the hanging slots, make a center line on the bracket backs. Then measure up ½" from the top back of the bracket and again at 1½".

With a hanging slot bit (H) in the plunge router, rout the hanging slot in each bracket.

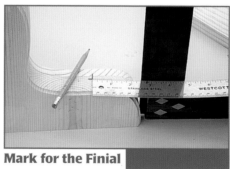

Mark for the Finial

Step 12 - To mark the location of the finial (C), measure up 1¾" from the lower end of the bracket.

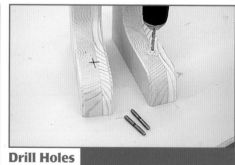

Drill Holes

Step 13 - Drill a 1"-deep hole where previously marked, using a ¹⁵⁄₆₄" drill bit (K).

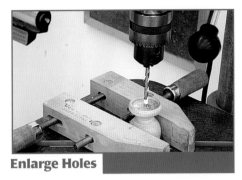

Enlarge Holes

Step 14 - Enlarge the hole in the finial to $^{15}/_{64}$", clamp firmly and drill 1" deep.

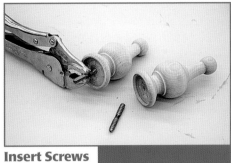

Insert Screws

Step 15 - Screw the dowel screws (I) into the finials. It helps to use a pair of vise grips (M) for this.

Sand all pieces through 220-grit sandpaper.

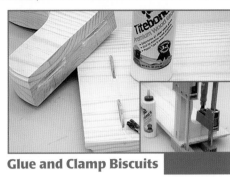

Glue and Clamp Biscuits

Step 16 - Using wood glue (J) and #10 biscuits (G), glue the brackets to the shelf. Clamp and let dry as shown in the inset.

Finish

Step 17 - Finish the shelf as desired. We used McCloskey Special Effects (L).

Screw on Finial

Step 18 - Screw the two finials onto the shelf.

Angels

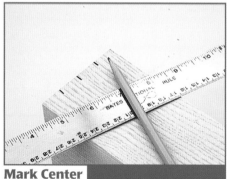

Mark Center

Step 1 - Cut the body blank (A) to the dimensions given in the material list. If necessary, laminate to achieve the 3" thickness.

Locate the center top of the body. Center a 1¼" space as shown.

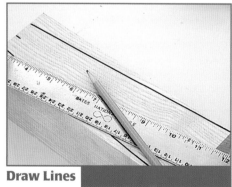

Draw Lines

Step 2 - Draw lines from the outside top marks to the outside bottom corners.

Turn the body once and repeat.

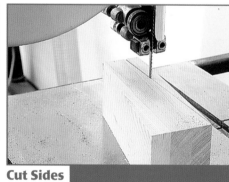

Cut Sides

Step 3 - Using a bandsaw, cut along the previously drawn lines as shown. Keep the cut offs!

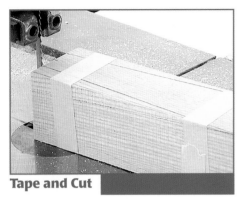

Tape and Cut

Step 4 - Tape the cut offs back onto the body using the masking tape (H). Cut along the lines on the second side of the body. Remove the tape.

Drill Top

Step 5 - Mark an X on the top to locate the center and mark with an awl (I). With a ¼" drill bit (J) in the drill press, drill a ½"-deep hole.

Material List		T x W x L
A body (1) (oak)		3" x 3" x 8"
B wings (2) (maple)*		⅜" x 8" x 9"
C small body (1) (oak)		2" x 2" x 7"
D small wings (2) (maple)*		¼" x 6" x 6"
Supply List		
E ball knob (1) (hardwood)		2" diam.
F ball knob (1) (hardwood)		1¾" diam.
G dowel (2)		½" diam. x 1"
H masking tape		
I awl		
J drill bit		¼"
K spray adhesive		
L wood glue		
M Forstner bit		⅞"
N Watco Danish Oil		
O candle insert		
P candle ring (bobeche)		
Q candle		5"

*See Pattern Packet.

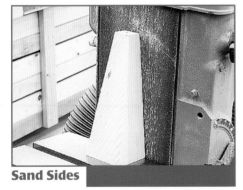

Sand Sides

Step 6 - Sand the body using a belt sander to first smooth the cut sides as shown. Then follow up with a hand sander sanding through 220-grit sandpaper, rounding top corners slightly.

Adhere Pattern

Step 7 - Cut the wing blank (B) to the dimensions given in the material list. Locate the wing pattern and adhere to the blank using a spray adhesive (K).

Drill Access Holes

Step 8 - Using the ¼" drill bit in the drill press, drill access holes in the pattern where indicated. Make sure to use scrap wood underneath to prevent tear-out.

Scroll Saw Inside

Step 9 - Cut out the inside of the pattern along the pattern lines using the scroll saw.

Scroll Saw Outside

Step 10 - Cut along the outside pattern lines using the scroll saw.

Sand the wings carefully through 220-grit sandpaper.

Glue Wings

Step 11 - Using wood glue (L), center and glue the wings to the body, clamping until dry. It helps to add the cut offs to get a straight surface when clamping.

Candle Holder

Step 12 - Find the center of the head (ball knob, E) and make a mark with the awl. It helps to clamp the ball knob in a wood vise as shown in the photo inset.

With a ⅞" Forstner bit (M) in the drill press, clamp the ball securely and drill to a ⅞"-deep hole.

Enlarge Hole

Step 13 - Enlarge the hole in the bottom of the head by turning the head over and clamping it in a wood vise. With the ¼" drill bit in the drill press, drill a ½"-deep hole.

Attach Head

Step 14 - Cut the dowel (G) to the length given in the material list.

Glue the dowel into the body at the neck and place glue in the hole in the head. Press the head onto the dowel. Let dry.

Oil Angel

Step 15 - Finish your angel with several coats of Watco Danish Oil (N). Or use a finish of your choosing.

Add Candle Insert

Step 16 - As an option, at this point you may place a candle insert (O) in the candle hole. If the fit is tight, it helps to place the candle insert in the hole and with a clamp ease the insert in as shown in the inset.

Add Candle

Step 17 - Place the candle ring (P) on top of the candle insert to prevent the candle wax from dripping onto the angel. Then add the candle (Q).

Country Plate Rack

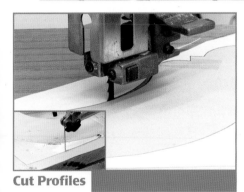

Cut Profiles

Step 1 - Cut the side and inner bracket blanks (A, B) to the dimensions given in the material list.

Locate bracket patterns (A, B). Adhere patterns to blanks using double-sided tape. Using a bandsaw, cut the profiles. Make the inner cut with a scroll saw as shown in the inset.

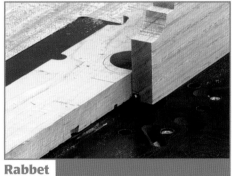

Rabbet

Step 2 - With a ¼" rabbeting bit in the router, rout a ¼" x ¼" rabbet along the inside back edge of the side brackets.

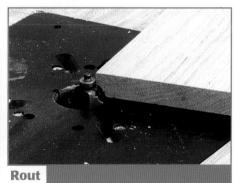

Rout

Step 3 - Cut the bottom (C) to the dimensions given in the material list. Using a decorative bit in the router, rout the front top edge of the bottom piece.

Pre-Drill

Step 4 - Pre-drill and countersink in the bottom blank for the inner brackets. Refer to the drawing on page 31 for placements.

Referring to the drawing on page 31 for dowel placements, mark and measure for the dowels.

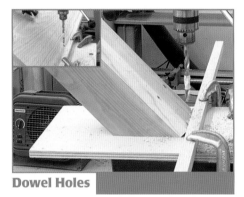

Dowel Holes

Step 5 - We used a 45-degree jig to hold our piece in place for this step. Clamp the bottom piece tightly to the drill press. Line up and drill a 1"-deep hole using a ⅜" drill bit as shown in the inset. Sand the bottom and sides through 220-grit sandpaper.

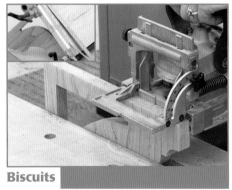

Biscuits

Step 6 - Dry fit and clamp the sides to the bottom. Measure in 1" from the front and back edge for biscuit (J) locations as shown in the inset.

Using a biscuit joiner, cut the biscuit slots in the edges of the bottom, and cut the slots in the inside edges of the side brackets.

Material List	T x W x L
A side brackets (2) (oak)*	¾" x 10¾" x 12"
B inner brackets (2) (oak)*	¾" x 10¼" x 11¼"
C bottom (1) (oak)	¾" x 10½" x 36¾"
D large plate rail (1) (oak)	¾" x 1¼" x 14⅝"
E small plate rail (1) (oak)	¾" x 1¼" x 11⅝"
F shelf (1) (oak)	¾" x 4" x 38¼"
G back (1) (oak beadboard)	¼" x 12¼" x 37¼"
Supply List	
H dowels (7) (oak)	⅜" diam. x 14"
I dowels (7) (oak)	⅜" diam. x 11"
J biscuits (6)	#0
K wood screws (4)	#6 x ¾"
L wood screws (6)	#6 x 1¼"
M plug cutter	⅜"
N decorative router bit	
O brads	⅝"
P Danish Oil	

*See Pattern Packet.

Glue and Clamp

Step 7 - Glue and clamp the side brackets to the bottom. Let dry.

Rails

Step 8 - Cut the large and small plate rails (D, E) to the dimensions given in the material list. Measure and mark for the dowel holes, referring to the drawing below for placement as shown in the inset.

Repeat the drilling method used on the bottom for both rails as shown.

Attach Brackets

Step 9 - Attach the inner brackets to the bottom by pre-drilling through the previously drilled holes in the bottom and attach using the wood screws (L) as shown.

Cut the shelf (F) to the dimensions given in the material list. Rout the front and side edges using the decorative router bit used previously.

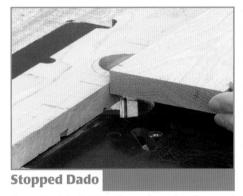

Stopped Dado

Step 10 - Mark ⅜" in from the side edges and rout a ¼" x ¼" stopped dado along the lower back edge of the shelf. Sand the shelf.

Use the biscuit joiner to attach the shelf to the side brackets. Refer to the drawing on page 32 for placement. Glue the biscuits and clamp until dry.

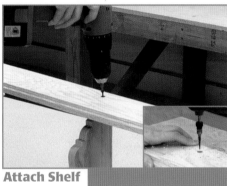

Attach Shelf

Step 11 - Where the shelf meets the inner brackets, measure in 1" from the back edge and countersink using a ⅜" bit. Attach the shelf to the inner brackets with wood screws (L) as shown.

Insert Dowels

Step 12 - Cut the dowels (H, I) to the lengths given in the material list. Set the dowels (H) into the large plate rail first. Place the dowels in the bottom piece, pushing carefully but keeping the rail flush with the brackets.

Repeat for the small plate dowels (I) and rail as shown.

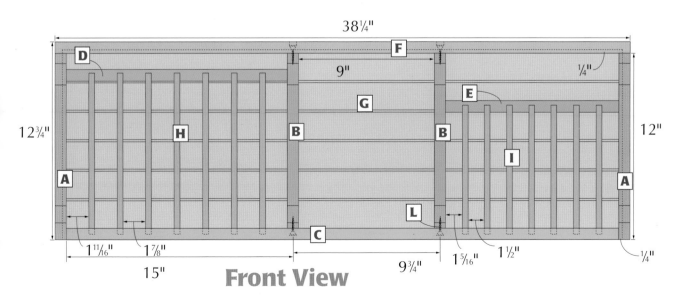

Front View

Attach Back

Step 13 - Cut the back (G) to the dimension given in the material list.

Set the back into the rabbet and using the ⅝" brads (O), attach the back, as shown.

Screw Back to Rails

Step 14 - Pre-drill and screw the back to the rails with wood screws (K).

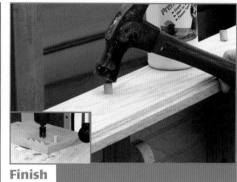

Finish

Step 15 - Using a ⅜" plug cutter, cut plugs for the shelf top as shown in the inset.

Glue the plugs in place and let dry. Trim the plugs with a finishing saw. Sand the project through 220-grit sandpaper.

Finish with several coats of Danish Oil. Let dry.

Exploded View

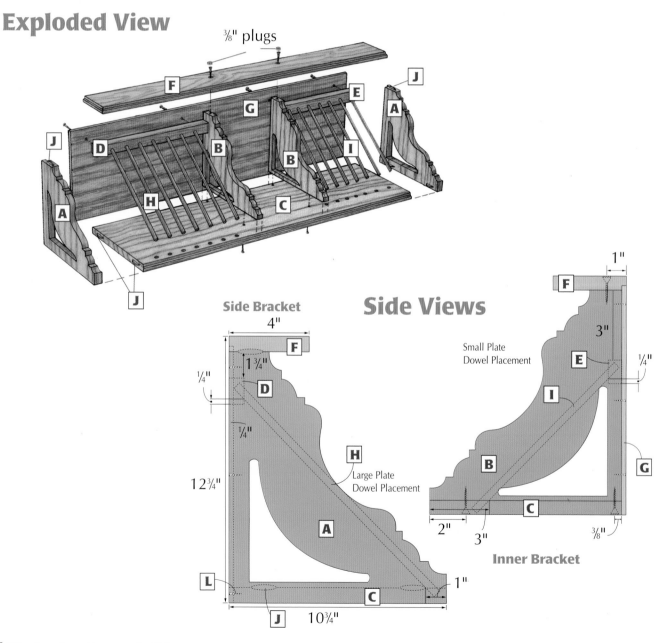

⅜" plugs

F, J, J, D, H, A, B, G, E, B, I, C, A, J

Side Views

Side Bracket

4"

1 ¾"

¼"

¼"

12¾"

F, D, H, A, L, J, C

Large Plate Dowel Placement

10¾"

1"

1"

3"

Small Plate Dowel Placement

¼"

F, E, I, B, C, G

2"

3"

⅜"

Inner Bracket

Wine Glass Holder

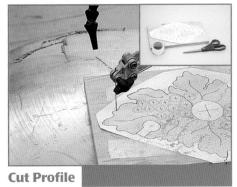

Cut Profile

Step 1 - Cut the holder blank (A) to the dimensions given in the material list.

Locate the holder pattern and adhere to the holder blank using double-sided tape (J) as shown in the inset.

Using the scroll saw, cut along the outside pattern lines as shown. Follow dotted lines across leaf; you'll cut this part out later.

Mark for Drilling

Step 2 - Mark the centers of all the circles on the pattern, using an awl as shown.

Center Hole

Step 3 - With the 1½" Forstner bit in the drill press, drill out the center hole as shown. Make sure you have a scrap board under your project to prevent tear-out.

Holes for Glass Stem

Step 4 - Place a ¾" Forstner bit in the drill press and drill the two holes for the wine glass stems as shown.

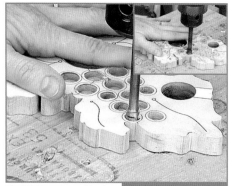

Drill Button Holes

Step 5 - To drill holes for the larger grapes (buttons), use a ½" Forstner bit and drill ¼" deep as shown in the inset.

The smaller of the grapes (buttons) are made using a ⅜" Forstner bit and drilling ¼" deep.

Material List	T x W x L
A holder*	½" x 7" x 10"
Supply List	
B screw hole buttons (14)	⅜"
C screw hole buttons (8)	½"
D Forstner bits	⅜", ½", ¾", 1½"
E drill bit	5⁄64"
F scroll saw blade (12.5 TPI)	#5
G wood glue	
H awl	
I Watco Danish oil	
J double-sided tape	
K 220-grit sandpaper	
L mallet	

* See Pattern Packet.

Scroll Saw

Step 6 - With a #5 blade (F) in the scroll saw, cut along the leaf line up to the ¾" holes as shown. Repeat for the other side of the holder.

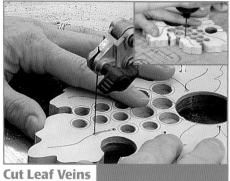

Cut Leaf Veins

Step 7 - Locate the access holes on the leaves and drill using a 5⁄64" drill bit (E) as shown in the inset.

To cut the leaf veins, put the scroll saw blade through the previously drilled access holes and cut to the end of the line pattern as shown. Back the blade up carefully and remove. Continue for each leaf vein.

Glue Buttons

Step 8 - Remove the pattern and sand through 220-grit sandpaper. Sand down the edges of the holder slightly and round the edges of the center hole.

With wood glue and a mallet, pound the screw hole buttons (B, C) in place as shown. Let dry.

Finish your wine glass holder with several coats of Danish Oil (I). Let dry and buff with a cloth.

Utensil Rack

Fill Adapters

Step 1 - Using the Quikwood epoxy putty (B) and following the manufacturer's instructions, fill the two copper female adapters (C) to the shoulder. Keep the bottoms flat as shown. Let the epoxy cure according to the directions.

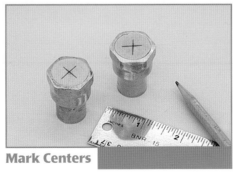

Mark Centers

Step 2 - When the epoxy is set, locate the center of the bottoms using a ruler and pencil. Mark the center with an X as shown.

Drill Centers

Step 3 - With a ³⁄₁₆" drill bit (E) in the drill press, drill through the putty in both adapters as shown.

Adhere Pattern

Step 4 - Cut the background blank (A) to the dimensions given in the material list. Locate the background pattern and adhere to the blank using spray adhesive (F) as shown.

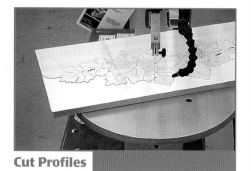

Cut Profiles

Step 5 - With a #5 spiral blade (G) in the scroll saw, cut the profile along the outside lines as shown. If you have a shorter bed on your saw, the spiral blade will make it easier to cut without having to turn the piece as much.

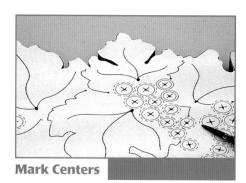

Mark Centers

Step 6 - Use the awl (H) to mark the centers of all the "grapes" as shown.

Material List	T x W x L
A background* (1) (Mississippi red gum)	½" x 11¼" x 22"
Supply List	
B Quikwood epoxy putty	
C copper female adapter	⅝"
D copper ell 90° street	⅝"
E drill bits	1/16", 3/16", 1/8"
F spray adhesive	
G scroll blades	#5 spiral, #5 skip tooth
H awl	
I Forstner bits	3/8", 1/2"
J abrasive cords	
K hanging slot bit	
L copper pipe	⅝" x 15¾"
M pipe cutter	#6 x 1¼"
N wood glue	
O wood buttons (walnut)	3/8", 1/2"
P Varathane water-based spray satin varnish	
Q round head machine screw	#6 x 1"
R washers	#6
S Wright's copper polish	
T nuts	#6

* See Pattern Packet.

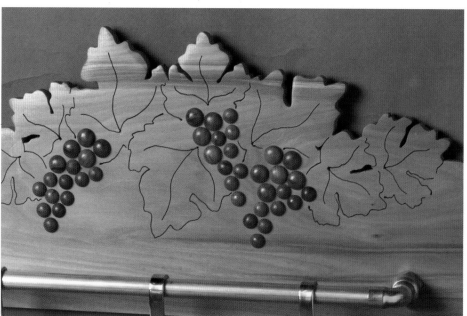

Drill for Grapes

Step 7 - With a ½" Forstner bit (I) in the drill press set to a depth of ⅜," drill all the larger holes marked on the pattern as shown.

Put the ⅜" Forstner bit (I) in the drill press. Set the depth stop to ⅜". Drill all the smaller holes marked on the pattern as shown in the inset.

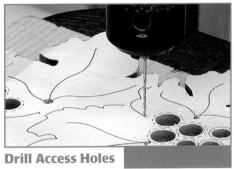

Drill Access Holes

Step 8 - Using a 1/16" drill bit (E) in the drill press, drill all the access holes marked on the pattern as shown.

Inside Scroll Cuts

Step 9 - Thread the #5 skip tooth saw blade (G) through an access hole and cut along the pattern lines, cutting out the black sections of the pattern as shown.

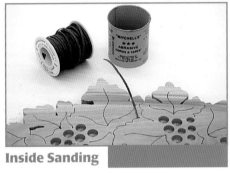

Inside Sanding

Step 10 - To help smooth the inside cuts, use an abrasive cord (J) threaded up through a cut as shown.

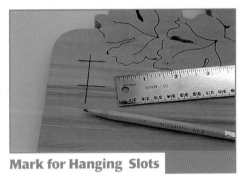

Mark for Hanging Slots

Step 11 - To make your marks for the hanging slot turn the plaque over and measure 1¼" in from both sides and mark. Measure up from the bottom 3" and 4" and make your start and stop marks for a 1"-long slot as shown.

Rout Hanging Slots

Step 12 - With the hanging slot bit (K) in the plunge router, rout the slot along marked lines as shown.

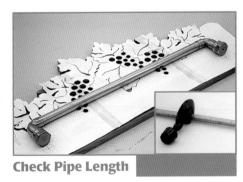

Check Pipe Length

Step 13 - Cut the copper pipe (L) to the length given in the supply list, using a pipe cutter (M) as shown in the inset.

Assemble, temporarily, the copper pipe, the copper ells (D) and the adapters to check the overall length of the rod assembly.

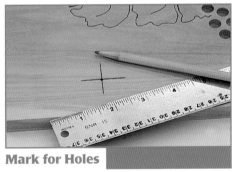

Mark for Holes

Step 14 - Line up the holes in the putty with the center marks on the pattern.

Mark through the pattern using an awl, or measure up 1⅗" from the bottom and 2½" in from the sides as shown.

Drill Through

Step 15 - With a ⅛" drill bit (E), drill a through hole where previously marked as shown.

Countersink

Step 16 - Put the ½" Forstner bit in the drill press. Turn the plaque over, and drill a ¼"-deep hole using the previously drilled hole as your center mark as shown.

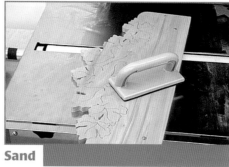

Sand

Step 17 - Sand the piece through 220-grit sandpaper. We used the Sand-Flee, a table top-drum sander, as shown.

Glue in Buttons

Step 18 - Using wood glue (N), glue in the ⅜" and ½" wood buttons (O) as shown.

Spray Varnish

Step 19 - Spray the piece with a few coats of an indoor water-based satin finish. We used a Varathane varnish (P) as shown.

Burnish

Step 20 - To get a nice smooth finish, burnish the plaque using a piece of brown paper bag as shown.

Thread Screw

Step 21 - Take a 1" machine screw (Q) and thread into the adapter from the top. Depending upon the thickness of your wood and putty, you might need to use a washer (R) as shown.

Polish Copper

Step 22 - Use a good copper polish (S) and polish the copper pieces clean as shown.

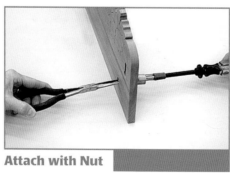

Attach with Nut

Step 23 - Attach the adapter to the plaque by threading the screw through the plaque. Hold the screw with a screwdriver, and put a #6 nut (T) on the screw. Hold the nut tight with needle-nosed pliers, and turn the screwdriver until tight as shown. Repeat for the other side.

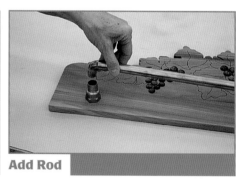

Add Rod

Step 24 - Place the ells onto both ends of the pipe. Set one end into the adapter; then set the other end. There is no need to solder this since no heavy items will be hanging on the rod.

Child's Chalk And Paint Easel

Basswood makes the milling in this project a dream. Removable trays help in storing.

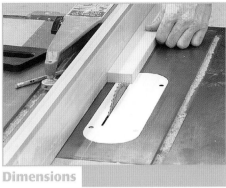

Dimensions

Step 1 - Cut the legs (A) and rails (B) to the dimensions given in the material list. Use the table saw to make the ripped cuts as shown. Use the radial arm saw to cut each piece to length.

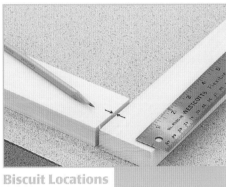

Biscuit Locations

Step 2 - The four rails are joined to the legs with biscuits. Locate the biscuit in the drawing on page 41. Locate where the rails are positioned. Mark for the R-3 biscuits (K) as shown.

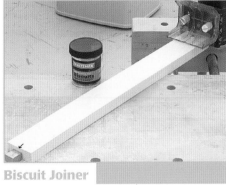

Biscuit Joiner

Step 3 - The R-3 biscuits are much smaller than the normal-size biscuits #0. Use a biscuit joiner that can make the proper slots in each rail and leg as shown.

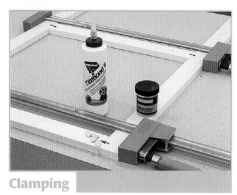

Clamping

Step 4 - Some assembly of the legs and rails is next. Place glue in all the biscuit slots and around the joining edges. Clamp the legs and rails together and check for square as shown.

Jointing

Step 5 - Before cutting the sides, ends, backs and bottoms for the two trays, joint one edge on the jointer as shown. This will give a better edge to run against on the table saw later.

Cross Cutting

Step 6 - Cut the fronts (F), backs (G), bottoms (H), sides (I) and inside shelf (J) to the dimensions given in the material list. Use the table saw to make the width cuts and the radial arm saw to make the length cuts as shown.

Material List	T x W x L
Body	
A legs (4) (basswood)	¾" x 2" x 43"
B rails (4) (basswood)	¾" x 2" x 20"
C locking arms (2) (basswood)*	¾" x 1½" x 12⅜"
D chalk board (1) (hardboard)	¼" x 19¾" x 20¾"
E paint board (1) (hardboard)	¼" x 19¾" x 20¾"
Trays	
F fronts (2) (plywood)	⅜" x 2⅝" x 23¼"
G back (2) (plywood)	⅜" x 2⅝" x 23¼"
H bottom (2) (plywood)	⅜" x 2⅝" x 23¼"
I sides (2) (plywood)	⅜" x 2¼" x 2⅝"
J inside shelf (1) (plywood)	⅜" x 2⅞" x 10⅜"
Material List	
K biscuits (8)	R-3
L round head screws (4)	#10 x 1¼"
M round head screws (4)	#10 x 1"
N flat head screw (1)	#10 x ¾"
O bulldog clip (1)	#4
P strap hinges (2)	2"
Q brads	⅝"
R wood filler	
S Minwax poly clear satin	wipe-on
T red acrylic	Delta Ceramcoat
U chalkboard paint	green

* See Pattern Packet.

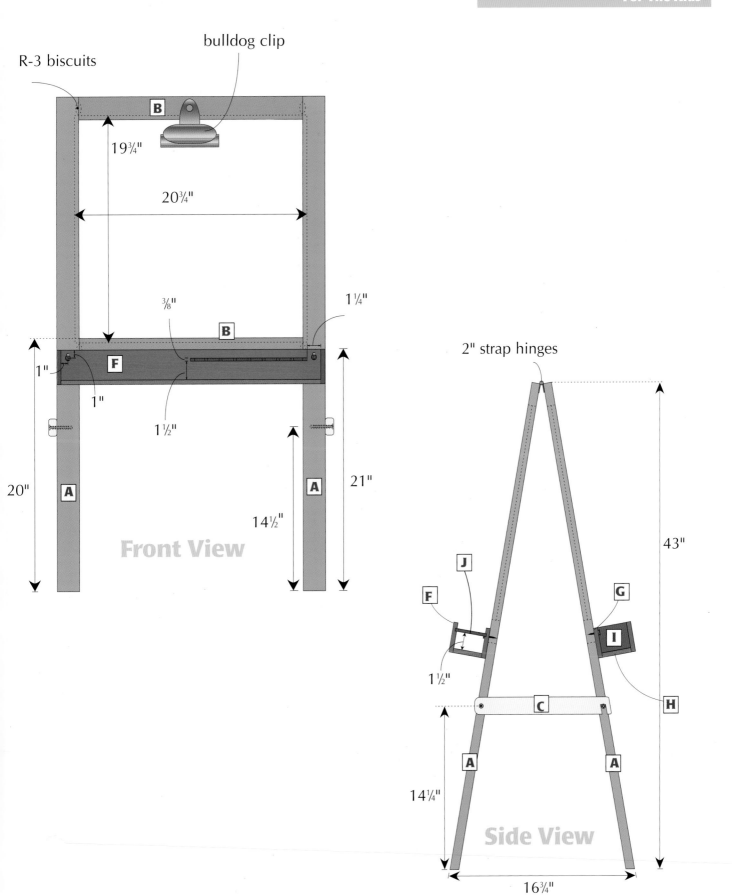

R-3 biscuits

bulldog clip

B

19¾"

20¾"

⅜"

B

1¼"

F

1"

1"

1½"

A

20"

A

21"

14½"

Front View

2" strap hinges

J

F

G

I

1½"

H

C

A

A

14¼"

43"

Side View

16¾"

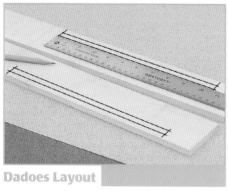

Dadoes Layout

Step 7 - The tray with the paints has an inside shelf to hold the paint tubes. The shelf is held in place by two stopped dadoes in the front and back blanks of the tray. Locate the position of the dadoes from the drawings on page 41. Mark each location on the two blanks as shown.

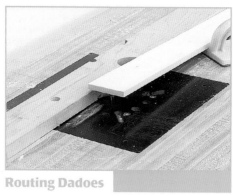

Routing Dadoes

Step 8 - Set the router table up to make the ⅜"-wide by ⅛"-deep stopped dadoes. Place indicator marks on the fence to show where your start and stop locations are. Plunge the blanks into the bit as shown.

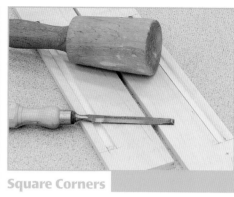

Square Corners

Step 9 - Using the router bit to make the dadoes leaves you with rounded ends. Use a sharp chisel and mallet to square up each end as shown.

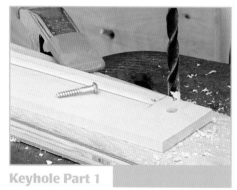

Keyhole Part 1

Step 10 - The trays are hung from the leg assembly through keyhole slots. Locate the hole locations from the front view drawing on page 41. Transfer the locations to the back blanks (G). Use a bit large enough to fit over the screw head (M) and drill the first through hole as shown.

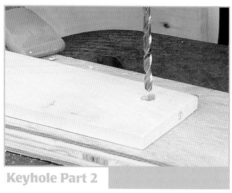

Keyhole Part 2

Step 11 - Using a smaller bit so that the screw head cannot fit through, drill the keyhole profile out as shown. Some adjusting might be necessary to smooth the keyhole out.

Inside Shelf

Step 12 - The inside shelf has a series of holes drilled into it. This step must be done after determining how many and what size tubes you will be using. Use a Forstner bit to cut out the circles as shown.

Tray Assembly

Step 13 - Now is a good time to sand everything through 220-grit sandpaper. Place a little glue inside the dadoes and along all the joining edges of the trays. Nail the trays together with the ⅝" brads (Q) as shown.

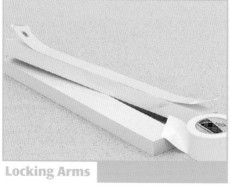

Locking Arms

Step 14 - Cut the locking arms (C) to the dimensions given in the material list. Locate the pattern and adhere to the blank. Gang the two blanks together with double-sided tape as shown.

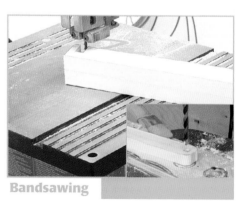

Bandsawing

Step 15 - Bandsaw out the profile of each locking arm as shown. Use the drill press to drill out the screw locations on the arms as shown in the inset.

Rounding Over

Step 16 - Before separating the two arms and having the arms stick out on the sides of the easel, it's a good idea to knock off the corners by rounding them over with the stationary sander as shown.

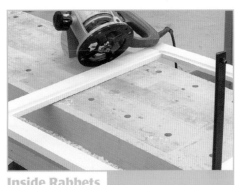

Inside Rabbets

Step 17 - On the inside of each rail and leg assembly, a rabbet is milled to hold the painting and chalk boards in place. Use a hand-held router and rout out a ⅜"-wide by ¼"-deep rabbet as shown.

Square Corners

Step 18 - For the boards to fit into the rabbets, the corners need to be squared up. Use a sharp chisel and a mallet to remove the material and square the corners as shown.

Outside Round Over

Step 19 - To protect the children from getting splinters, a slight round-over is placed on each facing edge. Use the hand-held router and a ¼" round-over bit to remove enough material to knock off the sharp edges as shown.

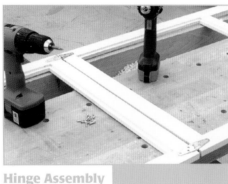

Hinge Assembly

Step 20 - The two rail and leg assemblies are held together with a couple of strap hinges (P). Place the two assemblies top edge to top edge with the inside facing up as shown. Use the barrels on the hinges as spacers between the two. Pre-drill and screw the hinges in place.

Chalkboard

Step 21 - Measure the board openings on the back of each leg assembly, and cut the chalkboard (D) and paint board (E) to the proper dimensions. Paint the chalkboard with green chalkboard paint (U) as shown. Paint the trays to a color of your choice as shown in the inset.

Arm Assembly

Step 22 - Locate where each locking arm is fastened to the legs in the drawings on page 41. Pre-drill and screw arms into place and latch screw as shown. Locate the four screws that hold the trays up in the front view drawing and screw into position as shown in the inset.

Finish

Step 23 - Three coats of a wipe-on poly (S) will greatly reduce the chance of paints and markers soaking into the wood and staining the easel. Apply each coat, let dry and lightly sand between each coat.

Fastening

Step 24 - After the poly has dried on the boards, place the chalkboard and paint board into their rabbets. Use the brad gun with ⅜" brads (Q) to fasten the boards in place. Screw the bulldog clip (O) in the center of the top rail on the painting side of the easel.

Hardwood Train And Shelf

Whether this train and shelf set is hanging in a collector's office or your child's room, it's great to look at and always fun to play with.

The Train

Although this train was made using mostly hardwood scraps and dowels, it can, of course, be made using any type of wood readily available to you. Paint it, stain it or just seal it. If a small child will be playing with it, make sure the finish is safe for kids.

Cut Bases

Drill Holes

Glue and Clamp

Step 1 - Cut the base and caboose base blanks (A, B) to the dimensions given in the material list. Locate the base pattern and make four copies. To save on cuts, gang together two blanks; repeat three times. Adhere the pattern to the blanks as shown in the inset.

Cut around the tongue area using a scroll saw as shown. Repeat for all bases.

Step 2 - Keep bases ganged, and with a ¼" drill bit (Z) in the drill press, drill through holes in each base set where indicated on the pattern as shown.

Sand smooth the curved and shoulder areas, slightly rounding the corners on all bases. Now separate the ganged bases and remove the patterns.

Step 3 - On three sets of bases, flip one base piece end-over-end and place on top of another base piece, matching corners. You should have a tongue at both ends. Separate the fourth set, pairing one with the caboose base. One will be a single base for the engine. Glue and clamp all bases until dry as shown.

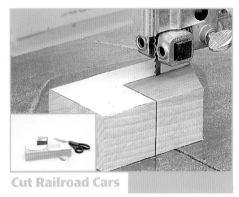

Cut Railroad Cars

Step 4 - Sand through 220-grit sandpaper until smooth.

Locate the patterns for the engine body (C), cowcatcher (D) and the coal car (J). Cut the blanks to fit the patterns, grouped or individually, as listed in the material list. Adhere the patterns to the blanks using double-sided tape (CC) as shown in the inset.

Use a bandsaw or scroll saw to cut along the pattern lines of each pattern as shown. Sand the edges of the engine, coal car and cowcatcher.

Glue to Bases

Step 5 - Glue the engine body to the single base. Clamp until dry as shown.

Material List		T x W x L
A	bases (8) (walnut)*	½" x 1½" x 5¼"
B	caboose base (1) (walnut)*	½" x 1½" x 4¼"
C	engine body (1) (maple)*	1½" x 2½" x 4¼"
D	cowcatcher (1) (walnut)*	1½" x 1½" x 1½"
E	engine roof (1) (spalted maple)	¼" x 2" x 3"
F	engine top (1) (walnut)	½" x 1" x 1½"
G	engine windows (2) (walnut)	¼" x 1" x 1"
H	engine front (1) (oak dowel)	1⅜" diam. x 2½"
I	engine small dowel (2)	¼" diam. x 1"
J	coal car body (1) (maple)*	1½" x 2" x 4"
K	coal car top dowel (1) (oak)	1" diam. x ¾"
L	logger dowels (3) (cherry)	¾" diam. 4"
M	tanker body dowel (1) (maple)	1½" diam. x 4"
N	tanker top dowel (1) (walnut)	⅜" diam. x 1"
O	caboose body (1) (maple)	1½" x 1½" x 3½"
P	caboose roof (1) (spalted maple)	¼" x 2" x 4½"
Q	caboose top (1) (walnut)	½" x 1½" x 3"
R	caboose windows (6) (walnut)	¼" x ¾" x ¾"
Supply List		
S	coupling pin dowels (4)	¼" diam. x 1⅛"
T	axles (11) (hardwood dowels)	¼" diam. x 2⅝"
U	toy wheels (22)	1½" diam. x ½"
V	smokestack (flower pot)	1¼"
W	headlight button	⅝" diam.
X	axle peg	¼" x 1¼"
Y	Forstner bit	1"
Z	drill bits	¼", ½", ⅜"
AA	wood glue	
BB	Special 'T' instant glue	
CC	double-sided tape	
DD	Watco Danish Oil	

* See Pattern Packet.

Sand Logs

Step 6 - Cut the engine front (H), logger dowels (L) and tanker body dowel (M) to the lengths given in the material list. Set the logger dowels aside. Sand a flat area along the engine front dowel and the tanker body dowel using a belt sander as shown to allow for gluing surface.

Drill Cowcatcher

Step 7 - To attach the cowcatcher to the front of the engine, mark the center front of both pieces. Drill a ¼"-wide by ½"-deep hole in the cowcatcher as shown in the inset. Drill a ¼"-wide by ½"-deep hole into the front of the engine body as shown.

Attach Cowcatcher

Step 8 - Cut the engine small dowel (I) to the length given in the material list and glue the dowel into the cowcatcher, spreading glue around the dowel as shown. Mate with the engine piece and let dry.

Drill Headlight

Step 9 - Mark the center of the engine front dowel as shown in the inset. Drill ⅜" deep, using a ½" drill bit as shown. Glue in the headlight button (W).

Drill Coal Car

Step 10 - Find the center of the coal car top and mark as shown in the inset. With a 1" Forstner bit (Y) in the drill press, drill on the mark ¼" deep as shown. Cut the coal car top dowel (K) to the length given in the material list.

Drill Tanker

Step 11 - Mark the center top of the tanker body dowel. With a ⅜" drill bit, drill a ½"-deep hole where marked as shown. Cut the tanker top dowel (N) to the length given in the material list.

Drill Engine Axles

Step 12 - Refer to the drawing on page 47 for axle placement on the engine. Mark for holes and drill through with a ⅜" drill bit as shown.

Drill Base Axles

Step 13 - Repeat step 12 with the remaining bases as shown in the inset photo.

Cut the caboose body (O) to the dimensions given in the material list. Sand the edges, rounding slightly on all corners.

Glue Cars To Base

Step 14 - Glue the car bodies to the bases using wood glue (AA). Clamp until dry as shown.

Cut Roofs

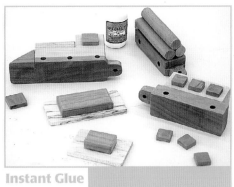

Instant Glue

Glue Coupling Pins

Step 15 - Cut the engine roof, top and window blanks (E, F, G) and the caboose roof, top, and windows (P, Q, R) to the dimensions given in the material list using a bandsaw.

Round the corners by sanding as shown. Sand pieces through 220-grit sandpaper.

Step 16 - Using Special 'T' instant glue (BB), glue the logs to the log car. Center and glue the tops to their respective roofs. Center and glue the windows to both sides of the engine and caboose as shown.

Step 17 - Cut the coupling pins (S) to the length given in the material list. Using wood glue, glue the dowels into the upper bases as shown. Pound the dowels flush with the top of the base.

Glue And Clamp

Drill Caboose

Drill Smokestack

Step 18 - Center and glue the roof pieces to the engine and the caboose as shown. Clamp until dry.

Step 19 - Mark the center of the caboose top as shown in the inset. Drill a hole with a ¼" drill bit, ¼" deep as shown.

Step 20 - Enlarge the hole in the smokestack (V) by clamping securely and drilling through using a ¼"-drill bit. Glue the engine small dowel (I) into the smokestack. The dowel should be flush with the inside of the smokestack/pot.

Axle Placements

Engine

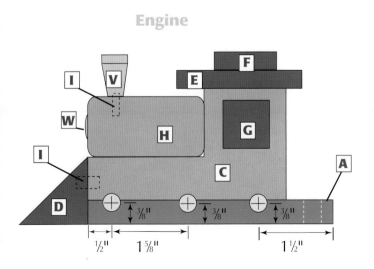

Flat Cars

Caboose

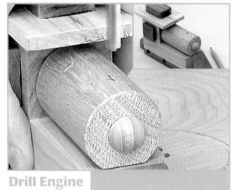

Drill Engine

Step 21 - Make a mark ¾" in from the front of the engine on the top of the dowel as shown in the inset. Drill into the mark with a ¼" drill bit ¾" deep as shown.

Add Dowels

Step 22 - Using wood glue, glue the coal car top dowel, the tanker top dowel, the caboose axle peg (X) and the engine smokestack in place as shown. Let dry.

Sand everything through 220-grit sandpaper one more time before adding the wheels.

Add Wheels

Step 23 - Cut the axles (T) to the length given in the material list. Glue one end into a wheel (U) so that the dowel is flush with the outside of the wheel. Slip the dowel through the axle holes and place a little glue on the end of the dowel. Push on another wheel until flush. Repeat for all axles and wheels as shown. Let dry and sand dowel ends if necessary.

Finish train with several coats of Danish Oil (DD) and let dry completely.

The Shelf

Use this shelf with or without the train. The selection of hardwoods is the key to separating the trees from the mountain. The woodgrain is vertical on the trees and horizontal on the mountain. If you don't have access to exotic woods, use stain for the different colors.

Rout Grooves

Step 1 - Cut the shelf (A) to the dimensions given in the material list.

Set up the router with the ⅜" core box bit (J); set to a height of ³⁄₁₆". Place a fence 1⅜" away from the center of the bit. Rout a groove along the back top of the shelf as shown in the inset.

Set the fence 1" away from the center of the router bit, and with the front edge against the fence, rout another groove along the front top of the shelf.

Material List		T x W x L
A shelf (1) (maple)		¾" x 4½" x 29"
B back/mountain (1) (exotic)*		⅜" x 8" x 29"
C sides (2) (maple)*		¾" x 1½" x 4½"
D brackets (2) (walnut)*		¾" x 4" x 4"
E bracket ties (4) (walnut)		½" x ¾" x 4¼"
F large tree (2) (walnut)*		¼" x 6" x 7"
G medium tree (2) (white oak)*		¼" x 4" x 6½"
H small tree (3) (exotic)*		¼" x 4" x 5"
Supply List		
I bracket dowels (4) (walnut)		¼" diam. x 2½"
J core box router bit		⅜" radius
K rabbeting bit		⅜" x ¼"
L wood glue (dark optional)		1"
M drill bit		¼"
N brads		1⅜"
O wood screws (4)		#6 x 1⅛"
P extension bit for driver		
Q hanging slot bit		
R Special 'T' instant glue		
S Watco Danish Oil		

* See Pattern Packet.

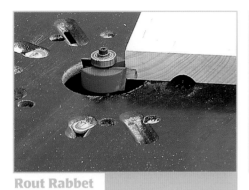

Rout Rabbet

Step 2 - Change the router bit to a ⅜" rabbeting bit (K). Set the height to ¼" and rout along the back top edge of the shelf as shown. Lower the router face plate and rout another ¼" out of the rabbet. Sand.

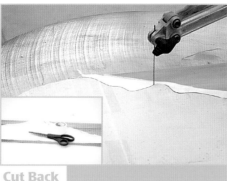

Cut Back

Step 3 - Cut the back blank (B) to the dimensions given in the material list. Locate the back pattern and adhere to the blank with double-sided tape as shown in the inset. Cut along the pattern lines using a scroll saw as shown. Sand the back.

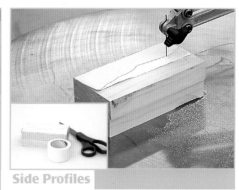

Side Profiles

Step 4 - Cut the side blanks (C) to the dimensions given in the material list. Locate the side pattern. Using double-sided tape, gang the two side pieces together and adhere the pattern as shown in the inset. Cut the side profiles along the pattern with a scroll saw as shown. Sand the sides.

Attach Back

Step 5 - To attach the back to the shelf, brush wood glue (L) along the rabbet. Set the back in the rabbet and clamp to hold as shown. Using a brad nailer and 1⅜" brads (N), evenly space brads across the back into the shelf as shown in the inset.

Attach Sides

Step 6 - Attach the sides to each end of the shelf with glue and brads as shown.

Use wood putty to fill the brad holes, let dry and sand.

Cut Brackets

Step 7 - Cut the bracket blanks (D) to the dimensions given in the material list. Gang the blanks together. Locate the bracket pattern and adhere to ganged blanks using double-sided tape as shown.

Pre-Drill Bracket

Step 8 - Using a bandsaw or scroll saw, cut the bracket profile along the pattern lines.

Cut the bracket ties (E) to the dimensions given in the material list.

Measure ¾" up from the end and from the inside corner. Center and mark. With a countersink bit in the drill press, pre-drill the brackets where marked as shown.

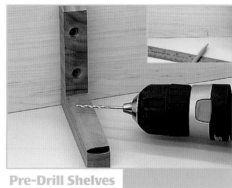

Pre-Drill Shelves

Step 9 - Measure in 7¼" from both ends of the shelf. Mark for bracket locations as shown in the inset. They should be 16" on center. Line up a bracket with a mark and pre-drill the shelf through the pre-drilled holes in the brackets as shown.

Line up the bracket tie so that the inside corners are flush with the outside edges of the bracket when placed on a 45° angle.

Drill Cross Braces

Step 10 - Mark for dowel placement on the bracket assembly. Center and mark ⁵⁄₁₆" from the end of the ties, and poke with an awl as shown in the inset.

Place a ¼" drill bit (M) in the drill press. Clamp the bracket assembly firmly and drill through all three layers where previously marked as shown.

Dowel Brackets

Attach Brackets

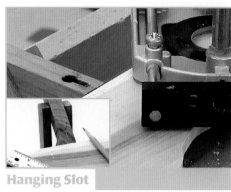

Hanging Slot

Step 11 - Cut the bracket dowels (I) to the length given in the material list. Put a drop of glue in the hole of the bracket and insert a dowel all the way through as shown. Let dry.

Using a finishing saw, cut the dowels flush with the bracket side as shown in the inset. Sand over the dowels for a smooth finish.

Step 12 - Attach the brackets to the shelf by spreading glue on the bracket and lining up the bracket with the pre-drilled holes. Using an extension driver bit (P), screw the bracket to the shelf using wood screws (O) as shown.

Step 13 - To make a hanging slot, turn the shelf over and measure ¾" up from the shelf on the bracket back as shown in the inset. Center and mark line. Clamp tightly to a workbench and with a hanging slot bit in your hand-held router, rout a ⅜"-long slot into the back of each bracket as shown. Sand off any marks.

Cut Trees

Place Trees

Mark for Glue

Step 14 - Cut the tree blanks (F, G, H) to the dimensions given in the material list. Gang the blanks together, three small, two medium, and two large. Locate the tree patterns and adhere the patterns to the appropriate blanks using double-sided tape.

Cut, using a scroll saw, around the ganged tree blanks following the pattern lines as shown. Sand all trees through 220-grit sandpaper.

Step 15 - Arrange the trees as desired. Use double-sided tape to hold in place as shown.

Step 16 - Turn the shelf around and use a pencil to draw a line along the back of the large and medium trees where they meet the back as shown.

Use Special 'T' instant glue (R) and spread glue under the traced line on the tree back as shown in the inset. Adhere the tree to the back, lining up pencil lines.

Glue and Clamp

Step 17 - Clamp until set as shown.
The small trees require glue on the tips that will overlap the trees behind. Hold until set as shown in the inset.

Finish with several coats of Danish Oil (S). Let dry.

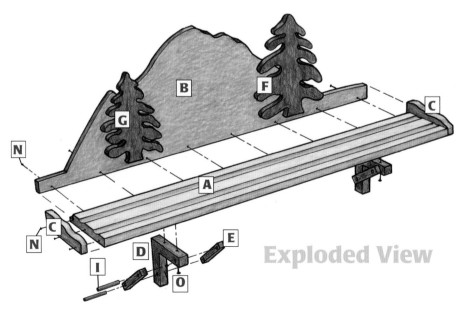

Exploded View

Child's Ball-Rolling Push Toy

It's a classic that's making a comeback! Only one screw is needed to put together this wonderful ball-rolling push toy.

Patterns

Step 1 - Cut the sides (A) and wheels (B) to the dimensions given in the material list. Gang the two sides and two wheels together using double-sided tape (N). Locate the two patterns of each blank and make two copies of each. Adhere a pattern to each ganged piece with double-sided tape as shown.

Band saw

Step 2 - Use the band saw to remove most of the material surrounding the sides, staying just outside the lines as shown.

Drum Sanding

Step 3 - To clean up the saw marks left behind by the band saw and to sand smooth to the lines, use the drill press chucked with a drum sander as shown.

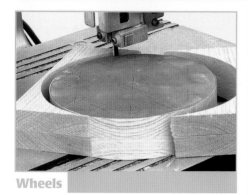

Step 4 - Use the band saw to remove most of the material surrounding the ganged wheels, staying just outside of the lines as shown.

Step 5 - Use the drill press with the drum sander to clean up any saw marks left behind by the band saw and to sand smooth to the line as shown.

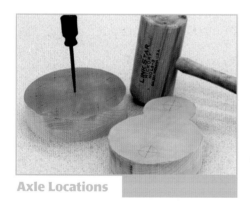

Step 6 - On each pattern there are hole locations for the wheels and for the sides. Use an awl to locate each hole on the material as shown. Separate the ganged side blanks and mark opposite holes.

Material List		T x W x L
A sides (2) (oak)*		¾" x 5½" x 7½"
B wheels (2) (oak)*		¾" x 6½" x 6½"
C axle block (1) (oak)		2½" x 2½" x 3"
D handle (1) (walnut dowel)		1" x 1" x 24"
E wheel axle (1) (walnut dowel)		1" x 1" x 10⅝"
F wheel spokes (12) (oak dowel)		⅝" x ⅝" x 9"
G handle axle (1) (walnut dowel)		1" x 1" x 10⅝"
H wooden balls (16)		1" x 1"
I handle grip doll head (1)		2" x 2"
Supply List		
J wood glue		
K wood screw		#6 x 1⅝"
L Provincial Stain (Minwax 211)		
M Watco Danish Oil (natural)		
N double-sided tape		

* See Pattern Packet.

Exploded View

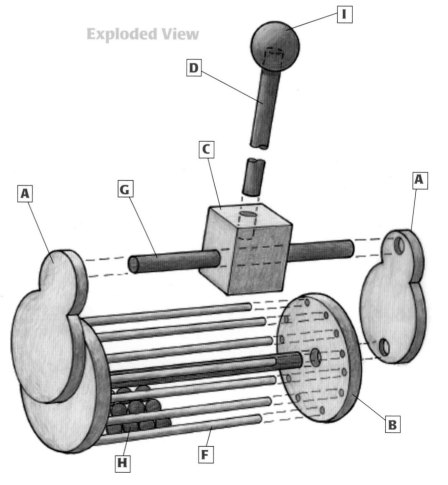

Side View

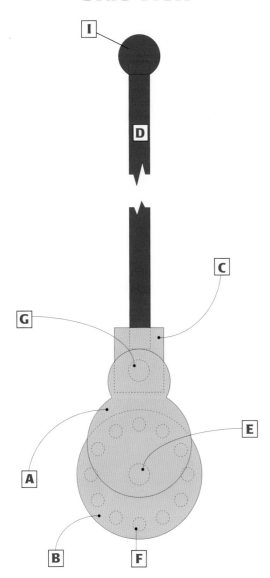

I

G

C

A

E

B

F

D

Front View

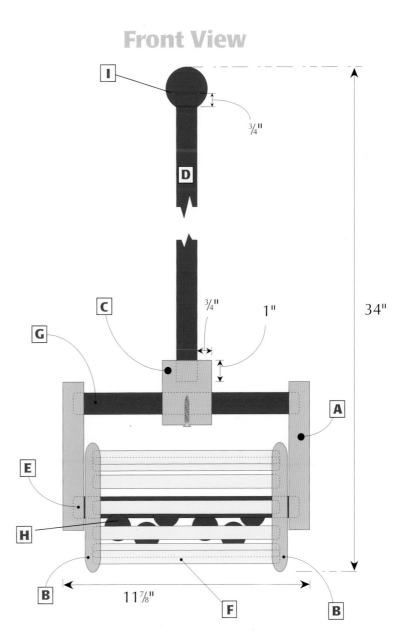

I

¾"

D

C

G

¾"

1"

34"

A

E

H

B

11⅞"

F

B

Axle Hole

Step 7 - Use the drill press with a 1" Forstner bit to drill through holes on the center location of the ganged wheel blanks as shown.

Side Holes

Step 8 - Use the drill press and the same Forstner bit in Step 7 to drill stopped holes to a depth of ⅜" where indicated with the awl tool in Step 6 as shown. Use the router table with a ¼" round-over bit to ease the edges on the outside of each side as shown in the inset.

Wheel Spoke Holes

Step 9 - Use your extra copy of the wheel pattern to mark each spoke hole location with the awl tool. Use the drill press with a ⅜" Forstner bit to drill the stopped holes to a depth of ⅜" as shown. Use the router table with a ¼" round-over bit to ease the edges on both sides of each wheel as shown in the inset.

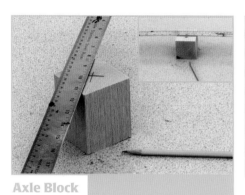

Axle Block

Step 10 - Cut the axle block (C) to the dimensions given in the material list. Locate the center on the top of the block as shown. Measure up from the bottom on one side 1". Center this mark as shown in the inset.

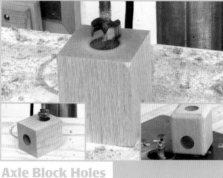

Axle Block Holes

Step 11 - Use the drill press with a 1" Forstner bit to drill the 1"-wide by 1"-deep hole in the top as shown. Use the drill press with the same bit to drill the through hole in the side of the axle block as shown in the left inset. Round over the block with a ¼" round-over bit on all edges as shown in the right inset.

Handle Axle

Step 12 - Cut the handle axle (G) and handle (D) to the dimensions given in the material list. Center the axle in the block and pre-drill through the block into the handle axle and fasten the two together with the wood screw (K) as shown.

Handle Grip

Step 13 - The handle grip (I) is nothing more than a 2" doll head , available at most craft stores. Clamp the grip into place. Use the drill bit with a 1" Forstner bit to drill the center location to a depth of ¾".

Wheel Assembly

Step 14 - Cut the wheel spokes (F) to the dimensions given in the material list. Glue and clamp the spokes into the wheels as shown.

Final Assembly

Step 15 - The sides are stained with Watco Danish Oil. The remaining pieces are stained with Provincial Stain.

Once all the pieces are dry, place the balls (H) into the wheel housing. Place the wheel axle and handle axle between the sides. Make sure the handle axle is straight up and down before gluing and clamping the entire assembly together.

Dragonfly Puzzle

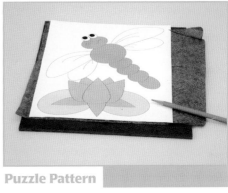

Step 1 - Cut the puzzle face (A) and the puzzle back (B) to the dimensions given in the material list. Set the back aside for later.

Transfer the pattern by layering the puzzle face frame (A), the transfer paper (C) and the pattern. Center and trace as shown.

Step 2 - Using a scroll saw, cut in from the bottom edge of the pattern for a starting point. Cut around the outside before cutting the individual pieces as shown. Place the puzzle face frame on the table and assemble the puzzle as you cut the individual pieces.

Glue Frame

Step 3 - Lift the puzzle face frame from the pieces. Turn over. Using wood glue (D), brush around the frame.

Place the frame onto the puzzle back and weigh it down until dry.

Material List		T x W x L
A puzzle face (1) (hardboard)*		¼" x 10" x 12"
B puzzle back (1) (hardboard)		⅛" x 10" x 12"
Supply List		
C transfer paper		
D wood glue		
E sandpaper (220-grit)		
F acrylic paints		
G spray gloss sealer		

* See Pattern Packet.

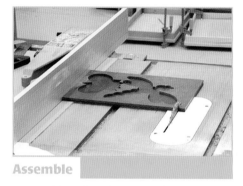

Assemble

Step 4 - Trim the edges to the finished size of 11" x 9" as shown. Sand the edges, rounding the corners. Assemble the puzzle and sand the top and sides lightly with 220-grit sandpaper (E).

Finish

Step 5 - Refer to the photo for colors and paint each piece as desired using acrylic paints (F) as shown. Let dry. Seal with the gloss varnish (G).

Puzzle Holder

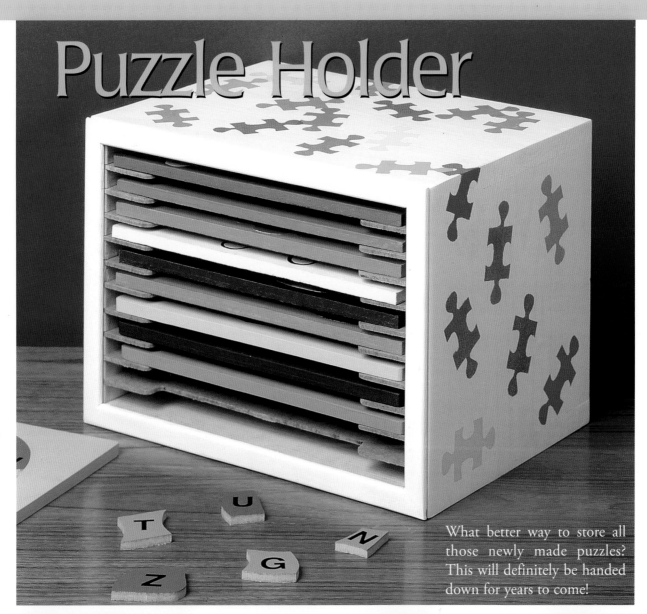

What better way to store all those newly made puzzles? This will definitely be handed down for years to come!

Dadoes

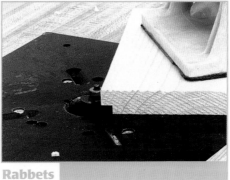

Rabbets

Stopped Rabbet

Step 1 - Cut the sides (A), the top (B) and the bottom (C) to the dimensions given in the material list. Referring to the drawing on page 59 for divider placements, measure and mark along the sides.

With the table saw blade set to a height of ⁵⁄₁₆", center the blade with a divider placement and run the side over the blade for the first dado. Continue to cut dadoes by lining up marks with the blade and moving the fence each time as shown.

Step 2 - Using a router and a ⅜" rabbeting bit (K), rout a ¼"-deep by ⅜"-wide through rabbet along the back inside edges of the side blanks, as shown.

Step 3 - Measure ⅜" in from the outside back edges of the top and bottom blanks and mark.

Rout a ¼"-deep by ⅜"-wide stopped rabbet along the inside back edges of the top and bottom as shown.

Clean up the corners of the stopped dado with a chisel (G) as shown in the inset.

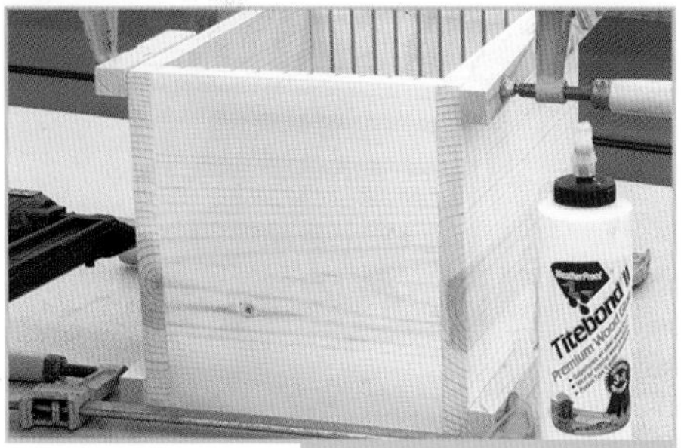

Assemble Box

Step 4 - Glue and clamp the sides to the top and bottom, using brads (I) and nailer (H) to help hold in place as shown. Let dry.

Material List	T x W x L
A sides (2) (pine)*	3/4" x 9 3/4" x 8 1/4"
B top (1) (pine)*	3/4" x 9 5/8" x 13 1/2"
C bottom (1) (pine)*	3/4" x 8 3/4" x 12 1/2"
D back (1) (hardboard)*	1/4" x 8 3/4" x 12 1/2"
E dividers (10) (hardboard)*	1/8" x 9 3/8" x 12 1/2"
F trim (4) (pine)	1/4" x 3/4" x 48"

Supply List	
G chisel	
H brad nailer	
I brads	1"
J wood filler	
K rabbeting bit	3/8"
L paint (American Accents by Rust-oleum) Heirloom White	
Aleene's Acrylic Paints	
M True Blue, True Green, True Red, True Orange, True Yellow, True Violet	

* See Pattern Packet.

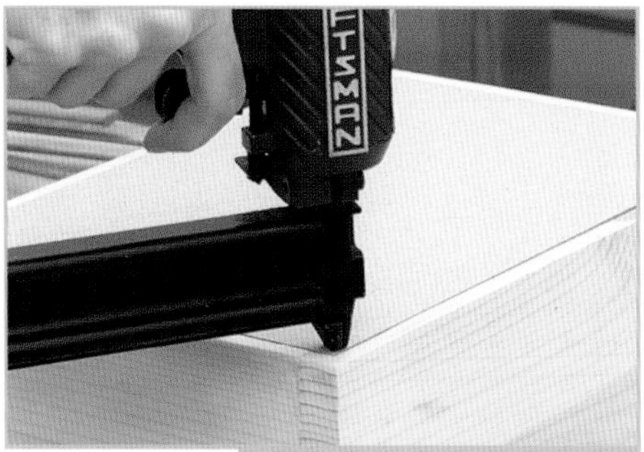

Attach Back

Step 5 - Cut the back (D) to the dimensions given in the material list. Set the back into the rabbets along the back of the box. Using the brad nailer, nail in place as shown.

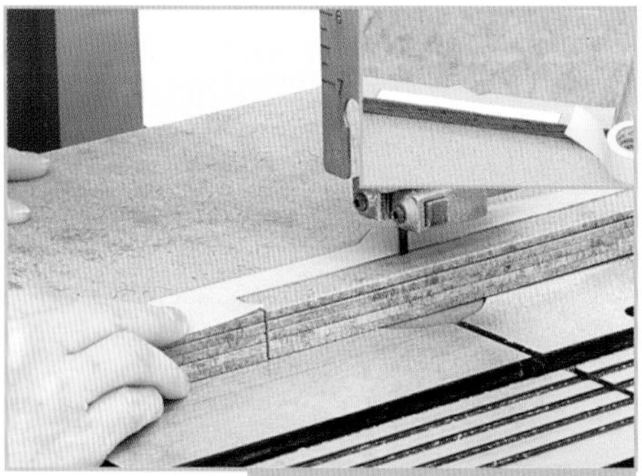

Cut Dividers

Step 6 - Cut the dividers (E) to the dimensions given in the material list. Gang five dividers together using double-sided tape, twice. Locate the divider pattern and adhere the pattern with double-sided tape to the front edge of the ganged blanks as shown in the inset.

Using a bandsaw, cut the divider profiles as shown. Repeat for the other ganged dividers.

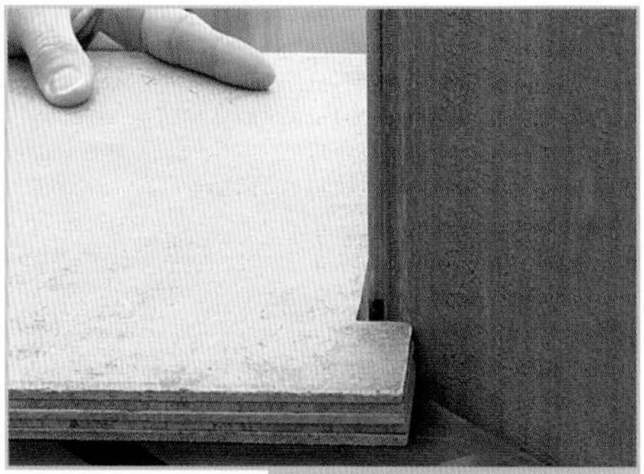

Sand Dividers

Step 7 - Round the corners of the cut profile using a belt sander as shown.

Slide the dividers into position in the box.

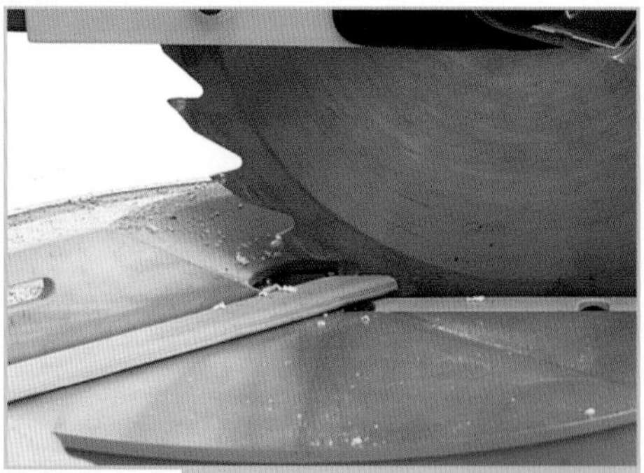

Cut Trim

Step 8 - Measure for the trim (F) along the top, bottom and side front edges. With a miter saw, set a 45-degree angle and cut the trim to fit your measurements as shown.

Front View

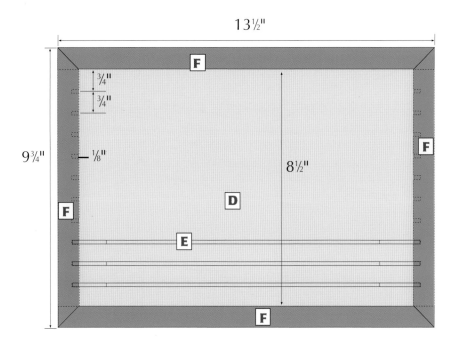

13½"

9¾"

8½"

¾"
¾"
⅛"

F D E F

Attach Trim

Step 9 - Glue and brad the trim to the front of the puzzle holder as shown.

Fill all brad holes using wood filler (J) and let dry. Sand through 220-grit sandpaper.

Paint

Step 10 - Tape off the dividers and with paint (L), paint the puzzle holder as shown. Let dry.

Finish

Step 11 - To make the puzzle stencil, locate the puzzle pattern and transfer to a sheet of thin plastic or cardboard. Cut the stencil out, using a craft knife. Using acrylic paint (M), stencil puzzle pieces randomly on the box.

Exploded View

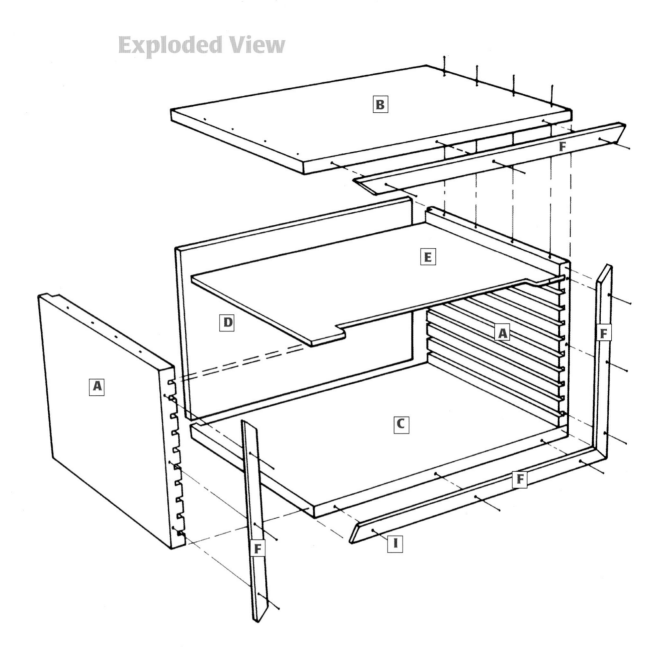

Potting Bench

Mark Half-Laps

Step 1 - Cut back bench support (A), upper and lower back rails (B, C) and back stiles (D) to the dimensions given in the material list.

A series of middle or T half-laps are used to join the stiles to the upper and lower back rails and to the back bench support. Laying out the pieces on the floor will make the marking job easier. Refer to the drawing and the piece drawings in the pattern packet for the half-lap locations and mark for placements as shown. The rabbet on the end of each stile is made on the front of the boards. The mating dado is cut into the back of the upper rail and bottom shelf support.

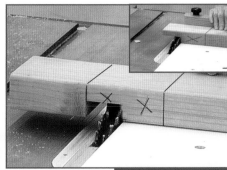

Upper Back Rail

Step 2 - Using a ¾" dado blade and a sliding miter table on the table saw, set the blade to a height of ¾."

Run the upper back rail (B) through the dado blade as shown, being careful to line up the blade with your marks. Repeat for other end of rail.

Cut the matching rabbet on the upper end of the back stiles (D) as shown in the inset.

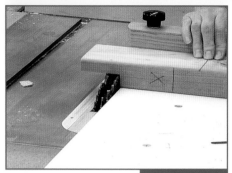

Lower Stile Half-Lap

Step 3 - Cut the back stile lower rabbet as shown. Repeat for the other back stile. Cut the matching dadoes in the back bench support (A).

Stile Dado

Step 4 - Cut the middle dadoes in the back stiles as shown.

Cut the matching rabbets on both ends of the lower back rail (C).

Material List		T x W x L
A back bench support* (1)		1½" x 5½" x 40"
B upper back rail* (1)		1½" x 3½" x 40"
C lower back rail* (1)		1½" x 3½" x 33⅜"
D back stiles (2)*		1½" x 3½" x 44¾"
E bottom shelf support (1)		1½" x 3½" x 40"
F back legs (2)		1½" x 5½" x 72"
G bench cleats (2)		1½" x 5½" x 4"
H bench side skirts (2)		1½" x 5½" x 21½"
I front legs (2)		1½" x 5½" x 32½"
J bottom side shelf supports (2)		1½" x 3½" x 19¾"
K bottom shelf boards (6)		1½" x 3½" x 40"
L bench front skirt (1)		1½" x 5½" x 46"
M bench back surface board (1)		1½" x 3½" x 40"
N bench surface boards (5)		1½" x 3½" x 47½"
O top shelf boards (2)		1½" x 5½" x 47½"
P top shelf board (1)		1½" x 3½" x 47½"
Supply List		
Q hanging plant brackets (2)		17"
R exterior deck screws		#6 x 1¼", #6 x 2"
S trellis (cut down to 60")		19½" x 72"
T copper tube strap (6)		¼"
U deck stain or sealer		

* See Pattern Packet.

Attach Stiles

Step 5 - Glue the back stiles to the upper back rail with wood glue and refer to the drawing on page 63 for screw locations. An easy way to mark for screws is to draw an X from corner to corner and measure in ¾" from the sides. Pre-drill and attach the stile to the rail using 1¼" screws (R) as shown.

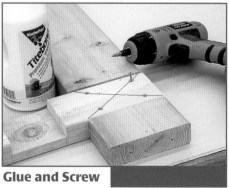

Glue and Screw

Step 6 - Glue the stiles to the back bench support. Mark for screws. Pre-drill and attach the stile to the rail using 1¼" screws (R) as shown.

Lower Back Rail

Step 7 - Repeating the previous step, attach the lower back rail to the stiles as shown.

Sand this center section through 220-grit sandpaper.

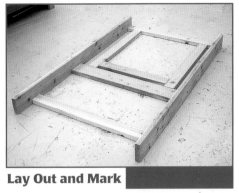

Lay Out and Mark

Step 8 - Cut the bottom shelf support (E) and the back legs (F) to the dimensions given in the material list.

Lay pieces out on the floor. Line up the center section with the top of the back legs and the bottom shelf support 6½" up from the bottom of the back legs. Mark for screw placements.

Attach Back Legs

Step 9 - Attach the center section to the back legs using wood glue and 2" screws (R) as shown. Attach the bottom shelf support to the legs as shown in the inset.

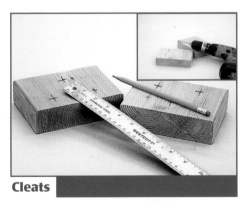

Cleats

Step 10 - Cut the bench cleats (G) to the dimensions given in the material list. Sand. Mark for three screws so that they do not interfere with screws used later; refer to the exploded drawing on page 65 for placements. Pre-drill cleats as shown in the inset.

Back View

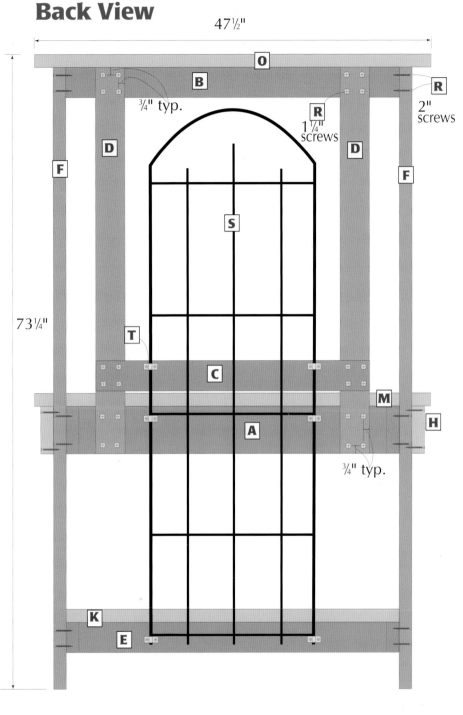

Attach Bench Cleats

Step 11 - Set the bench cleats on the back bench support against each of the legs. Attach the bench cleats to the back leg using wood glue and 2" wood screws as shown.

Attach Side Skirt

Step 12 - Cut the bench side skirts (H) to the dimensions given in the material list. Refer to the drawing for screw placement. Mark for screw placement, as shown in the inset.

Clamp side skirts in place. Pre-drill through side skirts into the back legs as shown.

Front Legs

Step 13 - Cut the front legs (I) to the dimensions given in the material list. Clamp the front legs to the side skirts and attach by gluing, pre-drilling and screwing through skirts into the legs with 2" screws as shown.

Bottom Side Supports

Step 14 - Cut the bottom side shelf supports (J) to the dimensions given in the material list. Mark for screw placement. Clamp the bottom side shelf support to the inside of the legs. Level, then glue and screw in place as shown.

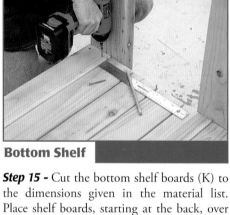

Bottom Shelf

Step 15 - Cut the bottom shelf boards (K) to the dimensions given in the material list. Place shelf boards, starting at the back, over the bottom shelf support. Use a screw between boards as a spacer. Pre-drill and screw in place as shown.

Attach Front Skirt

Step 16 - Cut the bench front skirt (L) to the dimensions given in the material list. Attach the front skirt to the side skirts by marking for screws, pre-drilling, gluing and screwing in place as shown. Clamp until dry.

Attach Bench Top

Step 17 - Cut the bench surface boards (M, N) to the dimensions given in the material list. Place the shorter board between the back legs, flush with the back bench support. Using screws as spacers, place the other surface boards with a ¾" overhang on sides and front. Refer to the exploded drawing on page 65 for screw placements; mark, pre-drill and screw boards in place as shown.

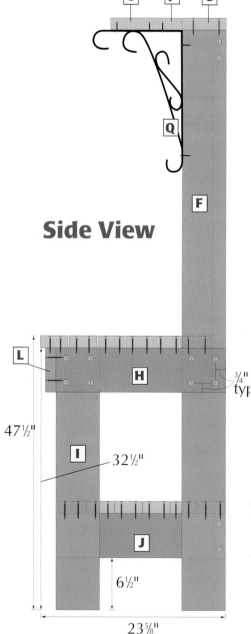

Side View

Hanging Shelf Bracket

Step 18 - Attach the hanging brackets (Q) to the front of the back legs. Making sure brackets are level with the top of the legs, pre-drill and screw the brackets in place, using 1¼" screws (R) as shown. (You might have to drill holes in your brackets depending on which brackets you buy.)

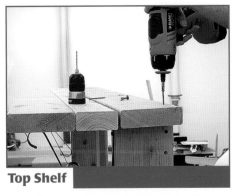

Top Shelf

Step 19 - Cut the top shelf boards (O, P) to the dimensions given in the material list. Place a 5½" board over the top of the legs, flush with the upper back rail and a 1¾" overhang on the sides. Using screws as spacers again, put the 3½" board in place, followed by the other 5½" board. Pre-drill and screw the boards in place as shown. Check exploded drawing for screw direction.

Attach Trellis

Step 20 - Using a hack saw, we cut 12" from the bottom legs and one butterfly off our trellis to make it fit. Center the trellis (S) on the back between the back stiles and clamp in place. Using copper tube straps (T), pre-drill and screw trellis in place as shown.

Sand the potting bench, rounding the edges. Finish with your choice of deck stain or sealer.

Exploded View

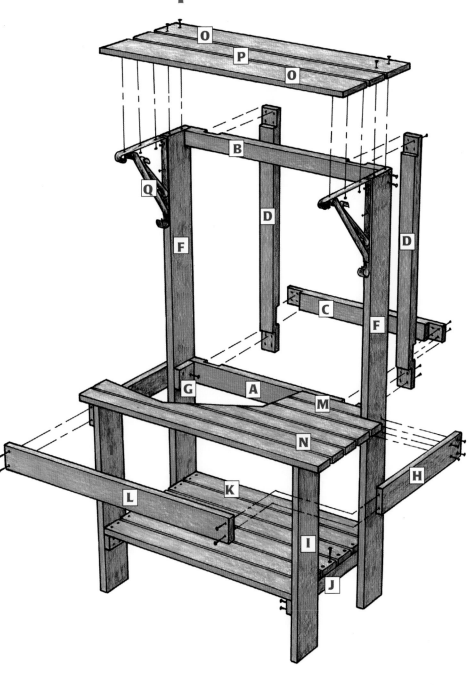

Seaside Bench

Dimensioning

Step 1 - Cut the top (A), side skirts (B) and legs (C) to the dimensions given in the material list. Use the radial arm saw and table saw to make the cuts as shown in photo and the inset.

Mark Dado Locations

Step 2 - The legs are secured in place by a couple of dadoes on the inside surface of each side skirt. Refer to the side view drawing for the ¾"-wide by ⅜"-deep dado locations. Mark each dado location on the side skirts as shown.

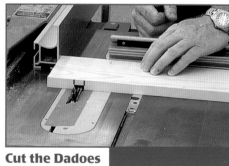

Cut the Dadoes

Step 3 - Use the table saw with a stacked ¾"-wide dado blade raised to a height of ⅜" and a miter gauge to make the dadoes in the side skirts as shown. Mark on the edge of the skirts the dado locations to give yourself a start and stop location.

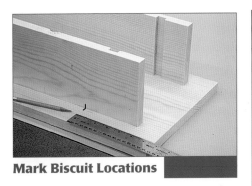

Mark Biscuit Locations

Step 4 - Three #10 biscuits (D) are used in each skirt to hold the top in place. Refer to the side view drawing for the biscuit locations. Transfer locations to the skirts and top as shown.

Material List	T x W x L
A top (1) (pine)	¾" x 11¼" x 36"
B side skirts (2) (pine)*	¾" x 5" x 32"
C legs (2) (pine)*	¾" x 9" x 20"
Supply List	
D biscuits (6)	#10
E wood glue	
F double-sided tape	
G wood buttons (4)	½"
H wood screws (4)	#6 x 1⅝"
Paints: McCloskey Distressed Wood Finish	
I distressed wood glaze cream (top coat)	#6455
J flat coat midnight blue (undercoat)	#6425
K paste wax	
L clear coat satin spray finish	#6280

* See Pattern Packet.

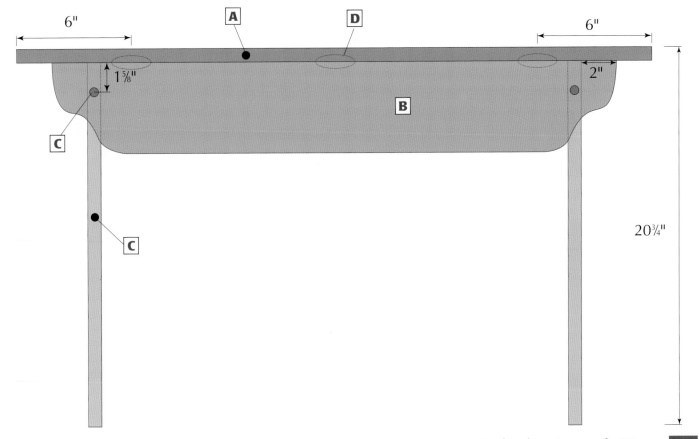

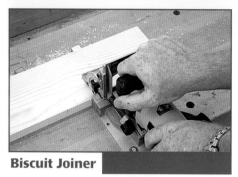

Biscuit Joiner

Step 5 - Use the biscuit joiner to make each slot in the side skirts as shown. For the top you'll have to close the fence on the joiner and make a top plate joint.

Apply Leg Patterns

Step 6 - Locate the leg pattern in the pattern packet. Make two copies, one for each leg, and save your original. Use double-sided tape (F) to adhere patterns as shown.

Cut Out Legs

Step 7 - Use the band saw to cut out the leg pattern profile as shown.

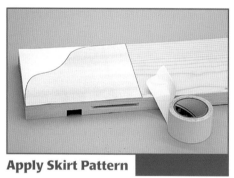

Apply Skirt Pattern

Step 8 - Locate the side skirt pattern. Make two copies and save your original. Adhere the patterns to one of the skirt's outside surfaces as shown.

Cut Side Skirts

Step 9 - Use the band saw to make the end profiles on the side skirts as shown. Trace the profile onto the second skirt, and repeat the bandsawing process.

Sand Legs

Step 10 - Use the drum sander chucked into the drill press to smooth the edges of the skirts and legs as shown. Use the drum sander to round over the sharp corners of the top.

Sand the entire project through 220-grit sandpaper.

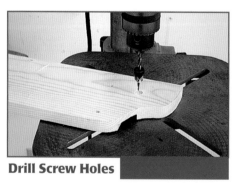

Drill Screw Holes

Step 11 - The legs also receive a screw through the dado on the skirts. Refer to the side view drawing for screw locations. Transfer locations to the side skirts and use the drill press with a ½" countersinking bit to countersink each hole to a depth of approximately ¼" as shown.

Round Over Top

Step 12 - Use the router in the router table with a ½" round-over bit to rout the top edge of the top piece. The round over is deep enough to make a small shoulder around the edges as shown.

Leg/Skirt Assembly

Step 13 - Place the side skirt's top end down on the table. Slide the legs into the dadoes top end down. Use the wood glue (E) in the dadoes, and fasten the skirts to the legs with the wood screws (H) as shown. Be sure to check for square as you proceed.

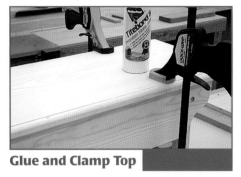

Glue and Clamp Top

Step 14 - Turn the project right side up. Place glue and biscuits into the slots of the side skirts. Place glue into the slots of the top, and clamp the top to the skirts as shown.

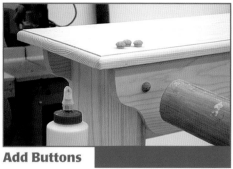

Add Buttons

Step 15 - Glue the wood buttons (G) over the screw heads in the side skirts as shown.

Sand the entire project through 220-grit sandpaper.

Side View

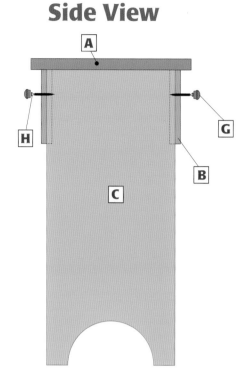

Apply Undercoat

Step 16 - The flat coat of midnight blue (J) is the undercoat. Paint the entire project as shown. Let dry thoroughly.

Apply Paste Wax

Step 17 - Apply the paste wax (K) to the areas you want to distress, most likely the corners and certain flat areas as shown. Be sure to follow the directions that come with each can.

Apply Top Coat

Step 18 - Paint the entire project with the distressed wood glaze top coat (I) as shown. Let dry overnight.

Spot Sand

Step 19 - Using 100-grit sandpaper, remove random areas of the top coat to reveal the undercoat as shown.

Finish

Step 20 - To protect the paint from normal wear and tear, apply a few coats of the clear coat satin (L) as shown.

See Pattern Page 1 for full-size patterns.

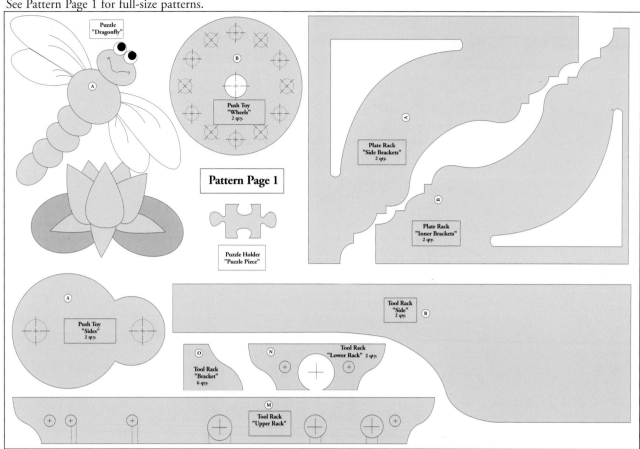

Puzzle "Dragonfly"

Push Toy "Wheels" 2 qty.

Pattern Page 1

Puzzle Holder "Puzzle Piece"

Plate Rack "Side Brackets" 2 qty.

Plate Rack "Inner Brackets" 2 qty.

Push Toy "Sides" 2 qty.

Tool Rack "Side" 2 qty.

Tool Rack "Lower Rack" 2 qty.

Tool Rack "Bracket" 6 qty.

Tool Rack "Upper Rack"

See Pattern Page 2 for full-size patterns.

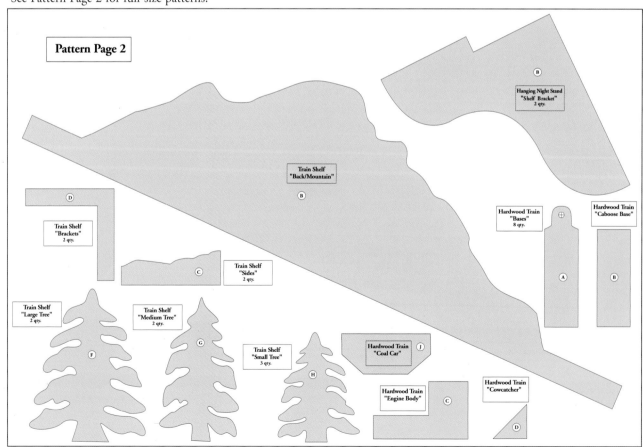

Pattern Page 2

Hanging Night Stand "Shelf Bracket" 2 qty.

Train Shelf "Back/Mountain"

Train Shelf "Brackets" 2 qty.

Hardwood Train "Bases" 8 qty.

Hardwood Train "Caboose Base"

Train Shelf "Sides" 2 qty.

Train Shelf "Large Tree" 2 qty.

Train Shelf "Medium Tree" 2 qty.

Train Shelf "Small Tree" 3 qty.

Hardwood Train "Coal Car"

Hardwood Train "Engine Body"

Hardwood Train "Cowcatcher"

See Pattern Page 3 for full-size patterns.

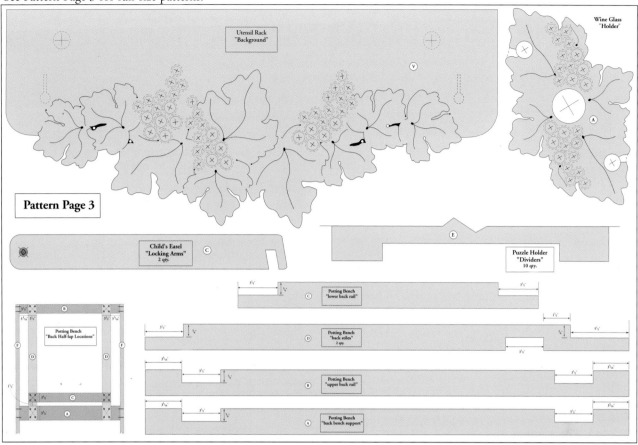

See Pattern Page 4 for full-size patterns.

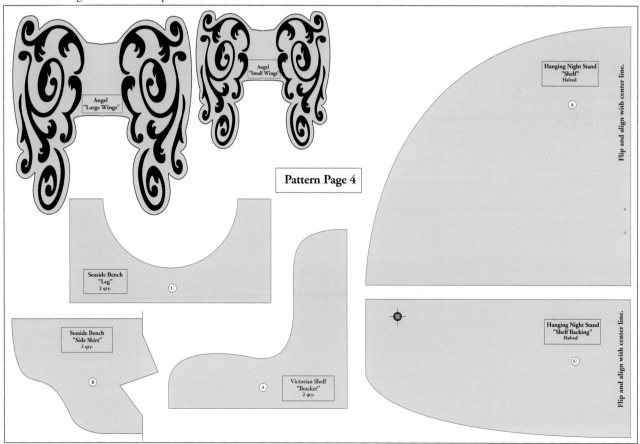

More Great Project Books from Fox Chapel Publishing

How-To Book of Birdhouses and Feeders
By Paul Meisel
This book features 30 birdhouse and feeder projects using common woodworking shop tools. Also includes information about attracting birds to your backyard.
ISBN: 1-56523-237-2, 208 pages, soft cover, $19.95

Intarsia Workbook
By Judy Gale Roberts and Jerry Booher
You'll be amazed at the beautiful pictures you can create when you learn to combine different colors and textures of wood to make raised, 3-D images. Features 7 projects and expert instruction. Great for beginners!
ISBN: 1-56523-226-7, 72 pages, soft cover, $14.95

Making Lawn Ornaments in Wood
By Paul Meisel
Stop traffic with these popular lawn and garden accessories. Features complete instructions and patterns for 34 projects, a full-color gallery and a paint mixing chart. Detailed instructions cover choosing the wood, transferring, cutting and painting.
ISBN: 1-56523- 163-5, 72 pages, soft cover, $14.95

Fireplace and Mantel Ideas, 2nd edition
By John Lewman
Design, build and install your dream fireplace mantel with this updated edition of a popular classic. You'll find step-by-step instructions for carving a rustic mantel and building a classic fireplace mantel, and an amazing selection of classic fireplace mantel designs like English traditional, Country French, Victorian, Art Nouveau, and more.
ISBN: 1-56523-229-1, 196 pages, soft cover, $19.95

Scroll Saw Workbook 2nd Edition
by John A. Nelson
The ultimate beginner's scrolling guide! Hone your scroll saw skills to perfection with the 25 skill-building chapters and projects included in this book. Techniques and patterns for wood and non-wood projects!
ISBN: 1-56523-207-0, 88 pages, soft cover, $14.95

Easy-to-Build Bookcases and Clutter Control Projects
By The Editors of Weekend Woodcrafts
Build it. Use it. Use your woodworking skills to create practical storage solutions for your home. From CD cases and end tables to potting benches and more, you will find projects to organize nearly every room of the house.
ISBN: 1-56523-248-8, 96 pages, soft cover, $17.95

Make Your Own Model Dinosaurs
By Danny A. Downs with Tom Knight
Everything you need to create exciting wooden dinosaur models–just like the ones in the museum stores! Inside you will find patterns and instructions for cutting and assembling seven different dinosaur projects. From the tyrannosaurus rex to the velociraptor, you'll find patterns for each and every dinosaur detail. Once all of the pieces are cut, share the fun with your friends and family.
ISBN: 1-56523-079-5, 112 pages, soft cover, $17.95

Making Doll Furniture in Wood
By Dennis Simmons
Learn to make hand-made doll furniture with the 30 projects featured in this book! Inside you will find 5 step-by-step projects for a bed, dresser, chair and more. You'll also find measured drawings for an additional 25 pieces of furniture. Projects are perfectly sized for American Girl® or any other 18" doll.
ISBN: 1-56523-200-3, 120 pages, soft cover, $19.95

Woodworker's Guide to Making Traditional Mirrors and Picture Frames
By John A. Nelson
A sourcebook of patterns for woodworkers that features plans for mirrors and frames. Learn the basics behind cutting wood for mirrors and frames, and then use the included measured drawings to create your own.
ISBN: 1-56523-223-2, 112 pages, soft cover, $17.95

CHECK WITH YOUR LOCAL BOOK OR WOODWORKING STORE
Or call 800-457-9112 • Visit www.FoxChapelPublishing.com